BACK UNDER SAIL

BACK
UNDER
SAIL

Recovering the Spirit
of Adventure

Migael Scherer

MILKWEED
EDITIONS

For Kit
Migael Scherer
2/12/05

Published 2003 by Milkweed Editions
Printed in Canada
Jacket and interior design by Christian Fünfhausen
Author photo by Paul Dudley
Maps and interior illustrations by Marilyn Perry
Alaska Native art of raven on p. 2 by Tresham Gregg
The text of this book is set in Requiem.
03 04 05 06 07 5 4 3 2 1
First Edition

An earlier version of "Raven Woman" appeared in *Sacred Bearings: A Journal on Violence
and Spiritual Life* (Virginia Foundation for the Humanities, Spring 2000)
and in *Connotations* (Island Institute, Spring 2001).

Portions of "Finishing Lines" were previously published in the essay "Mendenhall" in *Alaska
Passages: 20 Voices from Above the 54th Parallel*, edited by Susan Fox Rogers (Sasquatch Books, 1996).

Milkweed Editions, a nonprofit publisher, gratefully acknowledges support from the Bush
Foundation; Emilie and Henry Buchwald; John Cowles III and Page Knudson Cowles;
Dougherty Family Foundation; Joe B. Foster Family Foundation; Furthermore, a program
of the J. M. Kaplan Fund; General Mills Foundation; Jerome Foundation; Dorothy Kaplan
Light; Marshall Field's Project Imagine with support from the Target Foundation; McKnight
Foundation; Minnesota State Arts Board through an appropriation by the Minnesota State
Legislature; National Endowment for the Arts; Navarre Corporation; Debbie Reynolds;
St. Paul Companies, Inc.; Ellen and Sheldon Sturgis; Surdna Foundation; Target Foundation;
Gertrude Sexton Thompson Charitable Trust; James R. Thorpe Foundation; Toro
Foundation; United Arts Fund of COMPAS; and Xcel Energy Foundation.

Library of Congress Cataloging-in-Publication Data

Scherer, Migael.
    Back under sail : recovering the spirit of adventure / Migael
Scherer. — 1st ed.
       p.   cm.
    ISBN 1-57131-274-9 (hardcover : alk. paper)
    1. Scherer, Migael. 2. Women sailors—United States—Biography.
3. Sailboat racing—Alaska—Admiralty Island. I. Title.
GV810.92.S35A3 2003
797.1'24'092—dc21

                                                    2003006784

This book is printed on acid-free,
100 percent postconsumer waste recycled paper.

FOR MY HUSBAND:
my anchor and compass

BACK UNDER SAIL

ILLUSTRATIONS

AUTHOR'S NOTE

THIS IS SOMETHING you already know: At some point in your life you are weighed down, or loaded up, or knocked over. It may be a single, sudden event. It may be a series of events, one after another. Everyone's narrative is unique.

None of us knows how to navigate the changed world we find ourselves living in afterward. It's like a road trip without a map, a voyage without a chart—we don't understand where we're trying to go until we get there.

ARCTIC OCEAN

ALASKA

ANCHORAGE

CANADA

BERING SEA

ALEUTIAN ISLANDS

GULF OF ALASKA

SEATTLE

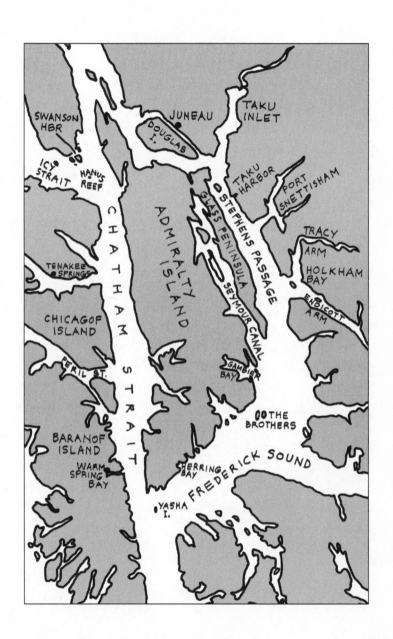

BACK UNDER SAIL

RAVEN WOMAN

RAVEN ENTERED MY LIFE through gifts.

First there was the sweatshirt, a present from my older sister on my thirty-sixth birthday. Turquoise blue, the color of glacier ice. On the front, a black raven painted in the graceful ovoids and swelling outlines of Alaska Native art: chest out, wings spread, tail fanned, head in profile. Surrounded by a thin black circle, with painted feathers hanging below.

"An eagle!" I said with pleasure when I unwrapped it.

"A *raven*," she corrected, pleased that I liked it. "The Tlingit bird."

I looked at the emblem more closely. Ravens were so common in Alaska that I'd pretty much overlooked them. I watched as she traced the soft contours that seemed to flow from one into the other, explaining how an eagle's beak would be more strongly hooked in Alaska Native art. When I put the shirt on, the raven covered my chest like a shield.

I wanted to save the sweatshirt for good, to wear it only on occasions that passed for dress up among us marina

3

liveaboards in Juneau, but it didn't take long for it to
join my everyday wardrobe. In the photo album of those
four years Paul and I lived in Alaska, I appear again and
again in that turquoise sweatshirt. At first I'm cooking,
or crowded with friends around the galley table, grinning
with them over a platter of salmon steaks. A few pages
later there I am, kneeling on deck, bending over a bucket-
load of Dungeness crab, orange rubber gloves on, ready to
kill and clean the whole lot of them.

The first blood to stain the shirt came off my friend's
halibut. We'd left the guys behind on *Orca:* Paul was launch-
ing the dinghy and rigging it for a sail. Herm was setting
up crab traps. Joyce and I took the inflatable.

We had fishing rods, herring for bait, a small tackle
box, a medium-sized net, and a club. Cans of beer rolled
around on the floorboards. We motored north about
a quarter mile, cut the engine, and dropped the plastic
bucket over the side to hold position. We baited our hooks
and dropped them to the bottom. Almost simultaneously,
we reeled up a few clicks.

And sat, Joyce on one inflated pontoon, I on the other,
beers open, smiles across our faces. Just us, the blue bowl
of sky, the sloping walls of the mountains around a calm
sea. To the south *Orca* floated on a tether of anchor chain;
the graceful sheer line of her hull swept up at stern and
bow, her masts raked gently aft.

Sooner than we expected, the tip of Joyce's rod curved
down to the water. She scrambled to grip the rod and
adjust the reel. I quickly reeled in my own line.

"Feels like a halibut," said Joyce. She was already

responding to the resistance of heavy flatness rather than
the darting fight of a salmon. She raised her pole up in a
slow pull, then lowered it quickly, reeling in furiously as
she did so.

Hauling in a halibut on sport line is often described
as raising a barn door: not elegant or tricky, but not easy
either. As they are with any fish, patience and pacing are
necessary, and stamina as well.

Joyce kept raising and lowering and reeling in, in a
steady pumping motion, not giving the fish time to dive.
Her line moved in circles as the fish moved this way and that,
trying to shake the hook caught in its throat, sawing the thin
monofilament with its sharp, fine teeth. Fighting for its life.

On the surface we were hooting and laughing. Our
beers had long since tipped and spilled onto the floorboards. Joyce was kneeling and I was sitting on the wet
bottom, oblivious to the cold sea-brew that wicked into
our jeans. I yelled unhelpful suggestions: "Keep the tip
up! Don't let it take any line!" Joyce grunted and giggled
in response. She was following her own instincts, reacting entirely to the halibut, as though receiving signals
through the translucent line.

When the ghostly form appeared below, we both gasped.
The halibut looked almost as big as the inflatable—much,
much larger than we'd expected. Its head wouldn't fit in the
net we'd brought, let alone the rest of it. We had no gaff to
hook it by the gills, no pistol to shoot it.

But we did have a handheld radio. As Joyce cautiously
gave the fish a little line, I called *Orca*. Could someone
bring the big net, soon?

It was the kind of challenge any boater would love—an emergency delivery of a large net for a large fish. Paul did it in style, hopping into the dinghy, raising the little sail, and beating his way upwind toward us. The small triangle of white sail and the wide circle of the aluminum net grew larger as he approached.

Joyce began to reel in again—the fish had rested and was resisting mightily. Paul pulled up on the opposite side, passed me the net and held onto the pontoon. I lowered the net into the water away from the struggling fish, then slowly brought it closer.

"Now!" said Joyce, and I swooped the net over and up with all the strength of both my arms. Joyce instantly let go of her rod and grabbed the rim of the net. Together we dragged the thrashing fish over the pontoon and into the boat, all but falling on top of it. Joyce raised the club and brought it down hard. Blood and slime splattered us both. The fish continued to thrash; I unsheathed my knife and plunged it through the halibut's brain.

We never figured out its exact weight. The best scale we could rig was to hang our stern anchor on the opposite side of the mizzen boom, and the balance seemed about equal—some sixty pounds. By the time we finished gutting and cleaning the fish, my sweatshirt was permanently stained.

In the logic of fishing, I treasured the raven sweatshirt even more now, a good luck charm I wore deliberately whenever I wanted to catch fish or crab. It never failed me.

ACCORDING TO NATIVE ALASKAN legend, Raven is power. Not the power that comes from size or strength

but the power that comes from cleverness and trickery.
Intelligence and deception are his weapons. Raven always
prevails. He helps man, but in an off-handed sort of way,
as much from a sense of fun as altruism. He is often pictured with the moon in his beak, a moon he acquired by
transforming himself into a crying, demanding child,
then released into the night sky. Raven is one of the most
admired of all animals, topping many a carved crest pole.
He carries none of the dreary associations of death and
carrion that I'd read in medieval ballads and Poe's grim
tales; in Alaska, Raven had more in common with the two
birds perching on Odin's shoulders in Norse mythology,
one named Thought, the other Memory.

Speaking realistically, it's difficult to describe ravens
in terms of nobility or grace. Their blue-black feathers
are elegant as satin and their profile is aristocratic, but
their walk is almost a waddle, and in flight they sometimes
tumble, as if they had suddenly forgotten how to fly. Their
cries are complex and harsh: quorks, tocks, rracks. They
have a greater variety of calls than any creature except
humans and they're skillful mimics. More than once I was
stopped on the dock by what I thought was a baby's cry
only to discover a raven, big as a rooster, peering down at
me from the rigging. Like crows, ravens often gather in
groups that seem to exist for play as much as work. They
have been known to tree cats, taunt small dogs, hunt in
groups. One Juneau story—reported with great flair in the
local newspaper—describes an Easter egg hunt thwarted
by ravens that had waited patiently while the colored eggs
were hidden; as soon as the humans were preoccupied with

registering the children, the ravens swooped in to collect over half of them, a six-hundred-egg bonanza.

What with the sweatshirt and my penchant for these stories, I was delighted when friends presented me with the gift of *Raven Woman* on my fortieth birthday. A signed print of a pen-and-ink drawing by an Angoon artist, it shows a realistic raven in profile, holding the moon in its beak. In front of the raven, obscuring its chest, is the face of a Native Alaskan woman. She stares straight ahead, with a look of complete calm and strength. The peaked band across her forehead is beaded with a raven shape very like the one on my sweatshirt. White feathers curve beneath her chin.

I propped up the picture in *Orca*'s main cabin and kept it there for weeks, then moved it to the forward cabin, and finally tucked it out of sight. That summer Paul and I cruised south, moving back to Seattle, and *Raven Woman* was forgotten. But the sweatshirt remained a vital item in my limited wardrobe. Photos of the six-week voyage invariably show me in that bright blue sweatshirt: walking a boardwalk trail outside Sitka, hopping to a jump rope of kelp on a British Columbia beach, standing watch at the helm on a sunny, downwind run.

THE DAY I SURRENDERED that raven sweatshirt, the blood on it was mine. The blood came from my hands and neck, from wounds inflicted by a knife much like the one I carried in my back pocket while fishing. The knife belonged to a man about my age, a quiet, blondish man who waited in a Seattle laundromat until I was loading wet clothes into the dryers. He attacked in a quick rush, knife to my throat, left arm like a steel cable across my body. He dragged me into the narrow room behind the dryers and raped me. Then he jerked the sweatshirt up over my face and strangled me. I don't remember seeing the shield of the raven then, but I saw the blue—that deep turquoise of a glacier crevasse.

I clawed uselessly at his wrists, his hands. I heard each breath as his thumbs pressed in and in—my breath, rasping, then retching. My brain was screaming, *I don't want to die!* but thinking too, rapidly and clearly, *How can I stop him?* In the furious scramble of my mind I suddenly remembered what I'd been told a thousand times in Alaska: When a bear attacks, play dead. And the moment I remembered— that very instant—I exhaled and went limp.

He unclenched his hands. "You're a lucky woman," he said, releasing me to the floor. I lay motionless, gasping, alive, grateful for air. A rustle of clothing, a slamming door, and he was gone.

So the last photos of me in the raven shirt were taken in the police station. And the last time I saw that shirt was on the witness stand. When I identified it as evidence during the trial, I recalled—just for an instant—halibut, crab, mountains and glaciers and clean, chill air. Then I saw the blood, dry and brown. I smelled the stale, soured sweat. Twenty feet away in that courtroom, the man watched as calmly as he had in the laundromat eight months earlier.

In the days that followed, while the trial continued, I remembered *Raven Woman*, retrieved her from storage, set her on a seat in the main cabin. The calm face of the

woman and the triumphant profile of the raven, holding
the prize of the moon in its beak, gave me a sense of peace
and hope that I desperately needed. I stared at that picture
every morning, woman and raven, the blackness of feathers and hair almost indistinguishable, her pale face like a
shield across its dark chest. It was a kind of prayer, my silence at that picture—through the rest of the trial, through
the relief of conviction, through the renewed anxiety of
sentencing a month later, and especially through the dark
depression that followed and nearly crushed me.

IT IS SAID THAT a totem animal chooses you as much
as you it, connects through a powerful event, bestows a
kind of grace. Thereafter, you are never the same.

CASTING OFF

The Spirit of Adventure Around Admiralty Island Race is held every summer solstice out of Juneau, Alaska. It's the longest coastal sailing race on the West Coast, a two-hundred-mile circumnavigation of a wilderness island, through the fjords of the Southeast Alaska archipelago. The race consists of two legs and takes about six days to finish, with a mid-course layover at Warm Springs Bay. International Yacht Racing Rules, with modifications, are used. A dozen or so Alaska sailboats of varying length and rig enter each year; a handicap system evens out competition between faster and slower boats.

Although few outside Alaska know about this race, Southeast sailors prepare for it all year. The main challenges in this remote setting are topography and weather. Channels and passages are rimmed with snow-topped, two-thousand-foot mountains that create unexpected wind shifts. Powerful currents accompany tidal ranges of twenty feet. Winds range from light and variable to major gales resulting in dismastings. Conditions change rapidly.

I LOOKED OUT THE SMALL, rounded rectangle of window, down at the patterns of water and land. The view from the airplane was a seamless chart, like the many we'd used as we cruised *Orca* south along that blue surface years ago. I counted back: Four years ago I was down there, not here in the air. The water that looked so flat from where I sat now, strapped in a narrow seat, had been three-dimensional and alive, responding with movement, color, and shape to the wind, the current, the terrain below the surface, and the atmosphere above.

I glanced at my watch; only an hour more, at most, until we landed in Juneau. I'd be sailing before sunset. The day after tomorrow I'd be racing. The Spirit of Adventure Around Admiralty Island Race—I wanted to say the name out loud. Unbelievable that I was doing this, at last, without Paul, just as I would have five years ago when Joyce had invited me to join the crew on her boat.

A clutch of regret and sadness. If only I hadn't been kept ashore by the flu; if only she hadn't been turned back by that storm. If only she were still alive, cancer a disease she'd fought to its death, not hers. I breathed deeply, in and out. So much unfinished at the end. Like a rope, cut and frayed.

The turbines droned and the anxieties I'd ignored in the excitement of leaving Seattle for Alaska enveloped me. Would I fit in with this crew? Joyce's had been all women; this would be all men. A week could be a long time on a thirty-four-foot sailboat with five men. I only knew two of them, and easygoing as they were, this would be a race, a competition. There was bound to be disagreement, could be a lot of yelling and barked orders. I felt my body stiffen. I'd raced before, but those were daylong contests at most, in full view of Seattle. Admiralty Island is wilderness, the race almost two hundred miles, the weather notorious.

I took another deep breath. *A woman's gotta do what a woman's gotta do,* I said to myself, but the joking reply was hollow. What was I was doing? Exploring? Escaping?

The hardest part of any voyage is pulling away from the dock. A thousand details ashore to settle, a thousand items to provision and check. Why should this be different? I thought of Paul, how he'd kissed me goodbye as if me leaving for an adventure without him was still a normal part of our long marriage. As if I hadn't been fearful and withdrawn and clingy for most of these past three years.

God, but I'd grown tired of myself. Tired of waiting for something: energy, hope, doom—whatever it was that would happen next. Tired of always looking over my shoulder, always holding back, observing my own life rather than living it. It seemed like the worst kind of defeat, to survive only to hunker down, pull everything inside, experience the world thereafter through a narrow opening, like a barnacle. Shouldn't I be stronger now, and brave? The thought of Joyce inspired me but shamed me too; dead over a year now, somehow she prodded me onto this plane, into this race.

"You're going to have a great time," Paul had said, as if the world was glorious.

THE PLANE'S SHADOW MOVED NORTH, its clean silhouette undulating as the terrain steepened. Past Ketchikan, mountains began to crowd the channels with jagged, whitened peaks. Less than an hour and a half ago

Seattle's web of streets and homes had spread out in every direction. Now I strained to find the signs of human settlement. A road writhed over gray-green slopes where clear-cut logging had left brown divots. A lone boat cut a trail over the water like a comet. The whitish mass of Petersburg hugged the north turn of Wrangell Narrows, as if being pushed by the wilderness into the sea.

EVEN WHEN PAUL AND I LIVED in Juneau and flew in and out fairly often, the descent into its airport always grabbed our attention: the banked approach from the north over Lynn Canal and Saginaw Channel, the rapid drop in altitude, and especially the way the mountains closed in. The runway below always looks far too short, and nearly is; the plane must touch down and come to a stop so quickly you're jerked forward, then back in your seat. It feels like being in a barely controlled crash. Once a flight attendant who was new to this run ended up on my lap, and many times when the fog was too thick or the winds too fierce the descent roar changed suddenly to a higher pitched ascent whine as the pilot aborted the land-ing. Newcomers complained about missed connections as the plane circled for another attempt, or as often flew back to Ketchikan or Sitka—sometimes on to Anchorage. But those of us who knew the dangers of this airport simply sighed. Even the most nimble jet with the most competent pilot could be slammed against mountains that were seconds away. The only safe course was to try another time.

On this day, in clear midsummer, the plane landed only

with its usual bump, bump, roar. I watched the spoilers on its wings splay upward to break our speed and ground us.

STEPPING OUT OF THE AIRPORT, I looked toward the Mendenhall Glacier and south toward Gastineau Channel. Isolated patches of snow clung to the creases of bright green mountains. The sky was blue, cloudless. There was dust in the air—dust! I peeled off my flannel shirt and hung it over my arm with my wool shirt. Unbelievable! I was in Juneau, I was warm, and I was dry.

Airplane pilots joke about finding Juneau: "Just head for the spot where the clouds are lowest." It may not rain as much as in Ketchikan (which averages thirteen feet per year), or even as hard, but for perpetual gray, wet days Juneau is the acknowledged champion. The usual summer weather report is forty degrees and raining. So rare is the sun that a beautiful spring day often results in offices closing up for sunshine liberty.

Now it was not only sunny, it was warm and windless. No thin chill from the icefields or penetrating coolness off the water. The temperature was easily in the high seventies. Everyone was grinning.

Days like these are a gift, and nobody wastes them. Those who can, leave work early; those who can't still enjoy a full day's worth of sunlight after work. It's summer solstice time—when the days are longest and the sun tracks across the sky in an elongated U, setting into a brief dusky twilight almost exactly where it rose. At fifty-eight degrees latitude Juneau isn't north enough for midnight sun, but on a day like today it will never be completely dark. Eight in the evening isn't too late to begin a hike or a baseball game.

I spotted Tim waving from his station wagon and hefted my bags. Inside the heaviest one was a survival suit—required for the Admiralty Island Race. In the other were a wool sweater, two turtleneck T-shirts, long underwear, wool hat, trousers, gloves, rubber boots, rain pants, and a float coat. Also, thank God, a pair of shorts I threw in for laughs, and a tank top.

Walking away from the crowd, I heard a hoarse croak and saw from the corner of my eye something black, unkempt, almost greasy. A pair of ravens, drawn as usual to human activity, were perched on the dumpster—my first genuine sighting this trip of Alaska wildlife. I knew I had arrived.

BY LATE AFTERNOON the temperature had risen to eighty-four degrees—a record high. The air-conditioning in Tim's car whined on its unaccustomed cold setting. As I pulled out of the parking lot at Foodland—my final errand—the local radio station was reporting that a power pole along Egan Drive had caught fire, apparently from oozing creosote that penetrated an insulator. The fire was out, but so was electricity in homes and offices north of downtown. *Hot!* The announcer was ecstatic.

When had such weather happened before? I could only recall one day in the four years we'd lived here. Paul and I had spent that afternoon picnicking on the silt "beach" of the Mendenhall Glacier. Even that massive river of ice seemed no match for the sun; we watched, amazed, as an enormous chunk, big as a church, calved from the glacier's blue-and-white face.

I was sweating lightly by the time I walked down the ramp of Harris Harbor with my sack of groceries. Odors collided in the warm air: the smoky resin of creosote exhaled by pilings and timbers, the sweet stink of living and dying creatures exposed at low tide, the tang of bottom paint on the drying hulls.

Most of the boats here could hardly be described as beautiful. They were rugged and stout, built for hard use. A few were derelict—whether temporarily or permanently, it was hard to tell. One wore a quilt of plastic tarps: orange, blue, green, and black. A long skirt of seaweed waved gently below its waterline. But on the whole these boats were cared for—not caressed into brightness like a yacht, but massaged and pounded into strength. Sanders, drill motors, and circular saws whined in competing pitches from every direction. Fresh white paint gleamed the length of gunwale and hull, spotting rough hands and muscled forearms. The owners and crew crawling over these boats were racing to get them rigged and ready for the next fishery, whatever it was. This would be the big year. This year they would plug the hold with enough fish to pay off all their debts and still have enough to buy the perfect boat that would make them rich.

The hopefulness infected me. I wasn't joining a crew to fish and make money but I was joining a crew. And it was like returning home, coming here to Harris Harbor. Paul and I had lived aboard *Orca* right there, on the end of that dock. Joyce's boat had been here, rafted next to Herm's.

The very give and sway of the floats under my feet made me smile; Macho Women we had called ourselves then, laughing, stomping the thick planks in our rubber boots.

I glanced back up the ramp, which was becoming steeper minute by minute as the tide went out. I stopped and listened to the timbers complain against the pilings, and the tiny mouths of countless barnacles click-clicking shut. And I remembered how I'd always checked the tide tables before hauling groceries or laundry, how I'd held tight to the rail in winter when the ramp was packed with snow. How in every season the rise and fall of water, twice a day, as much as twenty-three feet, was a giant pulse measuring our lives.

TIM WAS ON BOARD *Eagle,* engrossed in the solitary pleasures of readying her for sail. The covers were off, the winch handles were out, and all the hatches were open. "Check your shoes," he said when he saw me, his lean, sharp features softening impishly. "You can leave them on the dock."

Puzzled—it wasn't like Tim or any boater here to be fussy about their decks—I examined the sole of my left shoe. Gobs of black tar had stuck there, tar which under normal circumstances was absorbed into the heavy wood but which the rare heat had pulled to the surface. I glanced back along my route; even if I hadn't been so distracted on my way down the dock, I couldn't have avoided stepping in the sticky stuff.

I removed my shoes and socks and, for effect, rolled up my jeans. A barefoot sail under the snow-capped mountains appealed to me. I stowed the groceries below and joined Tim on deck.

"I put your survival suit with the others." He nodded toward the starboard seat and I lifted the lid to see for myself. The only suit labeled Small, it was easy to spot. The rest of my gear was still in his car; I'd spend the next couple of nights with Tim and his wife in their home across the channel.

Automatically I fell into working with Tim. Years of teaching together at the college, and weeks of cruising on *Orca,* had created an easy partnership between us. Tim was steady, unfailingly methodical, good humored in a pinch. He was the kind of person who could point out errors—in my programming code, say, or Paul's calculations from current tables—in a way that made you feel smart instead of dumb. And in that hard time three years ago, when I reacted to everyone on the basis of their response to my attack, Tim's was oddly perfect: a note card that pictured a cornered yet determined-looking kitten; inside, a long, newsy letter studded with offers of help ("even the tiniest little thing"), apologetic attempts to express his shocked dismay, and, in his second P.S., irrepressible enthusiasm for the coming Admiralty Island Race. His invitation this year to join *Eagle's* crew had made me feel—not confident exactly, not in the old way, but capable. Was that the word? Tim seemed to take it for granted that I would fit in and do my share, that I could handle whatever we encountered, and the very casualness of his assumption encouraged me to believe it as well. I liked these feelings, and liked being alone with Tim before the others came. I didn't know them as well; most of them I didn't know at all.

The rigging locker built into the cockpit seat was open, and *Eagle*'s polished stainless hardware blazed in the sun like jewelry in a treasure chest. More beautiful to me than jewelry, for every piece was a tool with a precise function that had been machined to snap or thumbscrew to a precise location. Every piece smooth as a wedding band inside and out.

Tim passed me a pair of blocks, his long, slim hands gesturing as gracefully now as they did through computer printouts, or over the keyboard of his piano. "This one clips to the fairlead track," he explained, pointing toward the toe rail that ran along the edge of *Eagle*'s deck like a tiny fence. "About halfway. And this one almost completely aft—that's right—to lead the genoa sheets."

There was a time when all this hardware would have com-

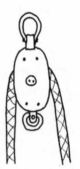

BLOCKS

pletely baffled me. It took me years, and real experience sailing, before I understood what everything was called, what it was for and how it all worked together. I had to learn that a rope isn't a rope, but a line. Then there are all the different kinds of lines: halyard lines that raise and lower sails (they haul yards of cloth, someone explained), sheet lines that control the sail once it's been raised. And different sheeting arrangements, depending on whether the sail is loose footed or boomed; loose-footed sails like genoas and jibs have two sheets, boomed sails generally have one. These lines are forever being adjusted as the sail is sheeted in and out, closer and farther away from the centerline of the boat, in order to be at a more efficient angle to the wind.

That's just the running rigging. There's also standing rigging and ground tackle, not to mention calling the front of the boat the bow and the back the stern, (or fore and aft); the right side starboard and the left port. The terms alone used to drive me crazy. Why not use regular words? The answer—precision and tradition—wasn't one I wanted to hear in my early teens. My irritation was really at my own ignorance, which was impossible to admit to my father, whose boat I first sailed and who had so little patience with any of us kids. He would simply repeat the word louder, the way someone will try to penetrate deafness—volume would explain it all. More often than not he'd take over the task we were fumbling through. "Not that line, the jib sheet, starboard! That's the main sheet!" By that time I'd forgotten what a jib was, and a sheet, and was on the verge of confusing starboard with port.

Despite all this (or perhaps because of it—I hated to feel stupid) sailing became a passion. Not that Paul was an easy teacher either. He didn't yell, but he was always explaining: the theory behind sailing, how an airfoil worked, about the Bernoulli Effect and vectors and wind shifts.

"So how did *you* learn to sail?" I threw the question into his face during one of our sessions in the dinghy. The conditions were ideal—light wind and warm sun—but between his explanations and my attempt to translate them into adjustments of tiller and sail we had stalled less than

a hundred yards from the dock. My patience with him and
with myself was about worn out.

For a moment he said nothing. We'd been married some
five years at this point, and certain patterns had already
set in. I'm testy when I fail at something new, and easily
discouraged, which annoys and amuses him. Which further
annoys me. Of course he heard the defiance in my question;
I expected him to fling it back now, with sarcasm.

Instead he looked at me and then across the water, as if
really considering my question. "I had someone breathing
down my neck and telling me what to do every second,"
he finally said. And then he winked, took the tiller, and
returned us to the dock. Before I could figure out whether
he was laughing with me or at me, he was out of the boat
and pushing me away. *What?*

"If you get into trouble," he hollered across the water,
"just lower the sail and use the oars!"

In that first minute alone I nearly capsized. Startled, I
released the sheet and nearly fell over the other way. Then
I went in circles, the boom swinging wildly as I cork-
screwed down the channel. My surprise at being pushed
off on my own flashed into anger, then alarm, then gradually turned into curiosity. Well, I was going *some*where at
any rate. If I let the sail all the way out with the wind at
my back, I could move fast and straight. That was easy.
It was going into the wind that was hard. Maybe if I just
controlled one thing at a time. I held the tiller still and
adjusted only the sail. Better. I shifted the tiller without
moving the sail. Better again.

By the end of the afternoon I was moving forward more

than backward and could change direction on purpose.
More solos in the dinghy and I learned to turn smartly,
to correct the heeling of the boat with my own weight, to
sail fast or slow, upwind or down. I learned to see where
wind touches the water and judge by the color there how
strong the wind might be, to feel its direction with my ears
and face. An artfully illustrated children's book helped
me through the technical terms of sailing, one at a time.
With a little reading and a lot more experience, I finally
understood how a boat could sail against the wind, how
to associate all the different lines with their uses, how to
break down even a complex rig into its simple parts. The
language of boats became my own.

I WAS HAPPILY UNCOILING *Eagle*'s soft, braided line
when Frank, Mike, and Larry arrived.

"Think we'll find any wind out there?" Frank set his
bundles on deck and, with the others, changed his shoes.
His voice boomed with pleasure. "Can you believe this
weather? I've never seen so much tar." Like everyone else,
he was grinning at the sun and sky, as if the air itself was
intoxicating.

Frank, who shared ownership of *Eagle* with Tim, was his
friend's opposite. Where Tim was lean, Frank was round,
with dark-rimmed glasses and a broad smile. Where Tim's
hair was straight and thin, Frank's was a mass of loose dark
waves. Tim had a preppie, tucked-in look about him, even
in his frayed jeans. Frank's clothing flapped loosely; it was
hard to believe he went to work in suit and tie, although
he did. And while Tim was newly married, and for the first

time, Frank and his wife had been together as long as Paul and I—over twenty years. Their youngest son, Mike, wore a smile like his dad's; all tanned youth and muscle, just out of high school, he shook my hand firmly when we were introduced, but his eyes were shy.

Larry, hair frizzled, seemed younger than I expected— probably in his thirties. Like Tim and Frank, he was totally at ease aboard *Eagle*. He didn't need to ask where anything was stowed and his feet seemed to know exactly where to step amid the lines and rigging. The three of them had been the core crew when *Eagle* won this race two years ago and when she placed second last year.

"Steve flies in from Seattle tomorrow," Frank explained when asked about his brother-in-law, our sixth crew-member. "Couldn't get away from work until then. It's okay. We can practice without him."

Disappointment flickered across Tim's face; Steve was the one person he didn't know. Frank squeezed himself into the starboard cockpit locker and disappeared into the engine room. He and Tim divided the maintenance tasks pretty evenly—the mechanical aspects were his respon-sibility, the sailing Tim's; underway, they alternated the position of captain.

Engine on, within twenty minutes we were away from the dock, past the breakwater and beyond the bridge that connects Juneau to Douglas Island. We cleared the cruise ships that rested tall and square at anchor, and in full view of the city Tim called out directions to raise sail. Mike leaped onto the foredeck to help Larry. I stayed aft to learn the cockpit work.

Eagle, a thirty-four-foot C & C, has a sloop rig, its single mast placed about a third of the way back from the bow. I watched the head of the mainsail rise up, then looked down to the foot of the mast, where Larry was wrapping the halyard around a small, gleaming winch that Mike cranked to take up the tension. The sail flapped above them.

"Sheet in the main," Tim said, pointing to the line that ran through a series of blocks and fairleads, then to a winch and cleat on the port side of the hatch. I pulled the line with my left hand and cranked with my right, then wrapped the line in figure eights around the cleat. Starboard of the hatch was one winch used by several lines—I'd need to pay attention there later. The jib and genoa sheets ran the length of the deck, aft through fairleads to large winches mounted port and starboard on the cockpit coaming; that was simple enough. But there were other blocks and fairleads that puzzled me.

"For the spinnaker," Tim said when I asked—a sail *Orca* doesn't have. But that was the least of the differences between *Orca* and *Eagle*. Everything here was smaller, lighter, faster. More lines to make more precise adjustments in sail shape. More sails: a jib, three genoas, a main, two spinnakers

25

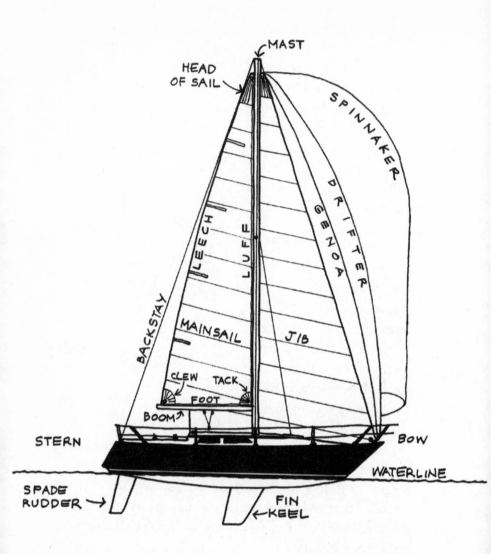

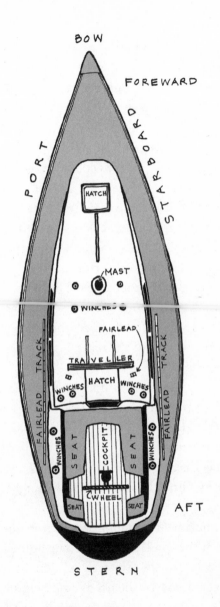

BOW

FOREWARD

PORT

STARBOARD

HATCH

MAST

WINCHES

FAIRLEAD

TRAVELLER

FAIRLEAD TRACK

FAIRLEAD TRACK

WINCHES HATCH WINCHES

WINCHES

WINCHES

SEAT

COCKPIT

SEAT

WHEEL

SEAT

SEAT

AFT

STERN

and a drifter. More combinations, potentially, than *Orca's* two-masted ketch rig.

And *Eagle* was vastly more responsive. With her fin keel and spade rudder, she responded as readily as a dinghy to the slightest sail adjustment. The light shell of her hull teetered with the shift of weight as we moved from side to side in the cockpit. She altered course at the barest touch of the wheel.

The wind was little more than five knots from the north, but it was enough for *Eagle*. "Let's go with the number 2," Tim said; that would be the medium-size genoa. "We need to see how this new mainsail performs."

Larry nodded from amidships. The genoa had been readied earlier, and he and Mike raised it now, like the main, while I took in the sheet. As the sail captured the triangle of air in front of the mast, *Eagle* immediately picked up speed.

That went pretty well, I thought, sitting back in the cockpit. Larry and Mike were sitting on the cabin, feet planted on the deck, knees up. I admired Larry's sure-footedness and liked the way he was quietly explaining *Eagle's* foredeck arrangement, and how Mike was listening, eager to learn. Fitting in with these guys might not be so hard after all.

Frank, who'd been watching us all from amidships, joined Tim at the wheel. He scowled up at the mainsail. "I hate to say it, Tim, but she feels—I don't know—it's not what I expected. Maybe she needs adjusting somewhere." And here I'd thought *Eagle* was practically trotting; in this wind, *Orca* would be at a slow walk.

"The luff looks about right," Tim replied. The edge of the sail against the mast was straight but not overly tight. "And the foot." There was a nice pocket along the boom. "Let out the leech a bit."

Frank fiddled with the twine on the long, outside edge of the main. He stepped back and shrugged.

"Maybe she just needs to stand a while," he said—the creases in a new sail can cause tiny areas of drag. "And Steve'll have some ideas."

My curiosity about our missing crewmember deepened. We'd been told he was an experienced racer; it was becoming apparent that more was expected of him than of the other three of us.

So we simply sailed south on a broad reach, the wind from the starboard side and slightly aft—the kindest sailing there is. It didn't feel like we were practicing, but we were. Like the new main, we were fitting ourselves to *Eagle* and to each other, moving into position, taking shape. For as much as a week we would be sailing, eating, and sleeping in a space smaller than most kitchens. On this, our first sail together, everyone was patient and deferential. We passed around sandwiches, scooted around in the cockpit, got in and politely out of each other's way. We learned the sounds of our voices and laughter.

The sky dimmed and the mountains seemed to move closer, dwarfing the lights of downtown Juneau. High above us, just out of sight, the icefields cast their strange, vanilla-colored light into a night that would never darken completely.

We continued south toward Sheep Creek. What was

usually, well into summer, a twisted wet ribbon flanked by packed, dirty snow was instead a waterfall. In the warm breeze I caught a whiff of something totally incongruous: cow manure?

"Our new sewage treatment plant," said Larry, noticing my squinched face. "The city promised we wouldn't smell it." He winked, and I smiled at the quiet joke.

"And we won't," said Tim, "if we come about. Helm's a-lee."

He turned the wheel to starboard until the bow pointed away from Sheep Creek. I slowly cranked the winch, sheeting in the genoa, as Larry sheeted in the main. Both sails moved inboard, their cupped shapes splitting the air, creating lift and movement like the wing of an airplane. *Eagle* headed back toward Juneau, tacking northwest into the soft wind, following the barely setting sun.

IT'S HARD TO IMAGINE a more unlikely place to build a city than Juneau. There's Gastineau Channel, barely a half mile wide, running roughly north and south— a perfect wind tunnel. To the west is Douglas Island, lumpy, thickly timbered, dominated by the ever-white peak of Mount Jumbo—a perfect trap for clouds. East of the channel is the almost vertical mainland: Mount Juneau and Mount Roberts glower like old men, their faces streaked with the scars of avalanches and mudslides. Between them is V-shaped Gold Creek Basin, and behind them lie fifteen hundred square miles of icefield. At times the frigid air drops to the channel so forcefully that the water is visibly depressed, as though punched by a giant fist.

In this geography, it seems like an act of reckless enthusiasm that Juneau is here at all. Which in a way is true; gold—one of the largest discoveries in the world at the time—muddled whatever good sense the prospectors had. Why else would grown men choose to build in such a cold, wet, avalanche-prone area?

Meanwhile, the Natives who told them where the gold was were living some eight miles to the north, where the fishing was better, the winds lighter, and it rained half as much. What miserable fools those prospectors must have seemed, cold and wet on top of their gold.

Cold, wet, and miserable: that about summed up how I felt the first winter we lived aboard in Juneau harbor. First came the October rain, one long deluge that fell sideways, night and day, a kind of sub-Arctic monsoon. After being soaked to the skin a few times on my walk to work, I took to wearing full rubber—jacket, pants, and boots. Like everyone else, I kept pressed shirts and dress shoes in office file drawers. The light slipped, minutes per day, into the dark of winter. The sky lowered.

Then came the slush season, temperatures hovering around freezing, just cold enough to snow and just warm enough to melt it. There were days when no plane landed and no mail arrived, weeks when everything on the barge that supplied the supermarket froze, leaving the lettuce brown and slimy, and even the carrots flaccid.

Fishermen say that one year in Southeast Alaska is worth three anywhere else when it comes to weather and wear on a boat, and the adage applied to me. I felt like a wimp, not rugged enough to stand up to the slamming

winds, the incessant dampness, the sideways rain. In my
worst moments I felt Alaska was out to get me, to drive
me back south. I had to make an effort not to take the
weather personally—an effort that was as irrational as
it was necessary. I missed the comparative warmth and
dryness of Seattle and Puget Sound with a sentimentality
that surprised me.

Paul, on the other hand, thrived in Juneau. His fingers
didn't turn white handling wet mooring lines, as mine did;
the rain seemed to roll right off the thick nap of his hair.
His colds didn't turn into lingering, chest-racking bron-
chitis. Not once in those four years did I see him counting
off the months until May, when the weather turned. Not
once did he complain. If anything, the weather energized
him. Perhaps, being half Norwegian, the low clouds, the
narrow channels, and the crowded mountains were a
comfort to him. Who knows what triggers the feeling of
home? What I do know is that all the New Mexican in me,
which I had never considered so important before, rose up
against the climate. I thought often of my grandmother,
who had died the year we sailed to Alaska. Her long underwear had been passed to me—creamy wool, woven into
a pattern of tiny hearts, top and bottom. It became my
second skin. For the first time, I understood why she'd
complained almost daily after moving from Albuquerque
to Seattle: "¡Ay, qué frío!"

I could also remember how her complaining had worn
on my mother. If I gave in to bickering, wintering aboard
would be a grim business. So I did my best to keep my
spirits up. I took to describing Juneau as a terrarium: wet

on the bottom, green and drippy on the sides. I religiously
recorded every beautiful day by drawing a beaming yellow
sun in the corner of the calendar square. (The most I ever
drew in a year was ninety-six, and half of those sunny days
were in the dead of winter; one year the total was only
fifty-seven.) To chase out the gloom I kept white Christmas
lights up in the main cabin from Thanksgiving through
Valentine's Day. Along with everyone else, I referred to
my brown boots as Juneau slippers and to my raingear as
sieve-tex.

I'm pretty sure it was in appreciation of my efforts to
keep up a sense of humor that Paul made an architectural
drawing of me with two cross sections (at chest and ankle)
that identified all the clothing I layered outward from my
body core. At the chest was the wool underwear, a turtleneck, a sweater, an insulated jacket; at the ankle was the
wool underwear, a wool sock, a trouser-leg, a rubber boot.
The title block read: "Alaska Heat Retention Retro-Fit:
Migael's Formula."

In time I learned that the trick to living in Juneau was
to do as the prospectors had done: put on a determined
exterior—act as rugged as I could—and at the same time
delude myself into thinking that conditions weren't really
so bad. Like those early settlers, I'd been drawn to Juneau
by a spirit of adventure and had stayed on for the good
job and money. I pretended, as they must have, that certain realities simply did not exist. When I walked across
Egan Drive on my way home from work, I'd look north
up its four lanes and pretend that the road actually went
somewhere. Never mind that fewer than forty miles in that

direction was a bright red stop sign nailed to a tree at the edge of a forest that stretched to the Yukon. I wasn't really isolated by water and ice, I'd say to myself; I could actually drive from Juneau through Canada to the rest of the United States if I wanted to. Or walking into town, looking straight up to the top of Mount Juneau, I'd pretend I was a tourist visiting a quaint European mountain village, say in Switzerland. A tourist, after all, is expected to notice the drop-dead natural beauty, not the hassles or hazards.

The pretending worked, sometimes, but the evidence of my senses was stronger; reality prevailed. And even now, sitting next to Tim on our way to the skippers' meeting at the Breakwater Hotel, I felt vulnerable. Human habitation here is too precarious. A simple shrug, a slip of mud or snow, and the mountains could tumble everything—me, the frame houses, the cars and trucks, the solid-seeming office buildings—into the deep waters of the channel like so many discarded blocks and toys.

THE BREAKWATER HOTEL isn't slick or fancy. If anything, it's a bit worn, more of a working vessel than a yacht. Placed dead center in the avalanche zone, the two-story structure boldly puffs out its chest toward the harbor, as though ignoring the three-thousand-foot mass of Mount Juneau at its back.

The expected decor: a huge anchor at the entrance, a giant ship's wheel in the lobby. A staircase that appears to lead to captain's quarters ascends to a restaurant and bar where, I knew, raingear and work boots were acceptable attire.

I followed Tim down concrete stairs to the basement and into a conference room noisy with talk and laughter. The Juneau Sailing Club had already been through its spring series of races and everyone seemed to know one another. For a moment I was caught off guard by all the new faces, then reminded myself that Paul and I had never joined this club; a fat, heavy boat like *Orca* was hardly a racer.

Frank was sitting toward the far end of the table, all gesture and talk. Next to him was a fit, tan, clean-shaven man who looked like he had sprung, full grown, from a Land's End catalog: Steve, our sixth crew member. As we shook hands, Steve handed me a navy blue cotton baseball cap with "Eagle" embroidered in red on the crown. It was a gift, clearly, but so casually given that it didn't feel like one.

"Thanks," I said, fingering the raised thread. But when I looked up, the three men were already huddled into their own conversation.

I winced. I'm used to being ignored by men when they're discussing "serious" subjects. It's rare to be deferred to or listened to, even rarer to be asked for an opinion. Compared to most of the people in the room—overwhelmingly male, but nothing unusual about that—I was a novice racer. Okay. But the feeling that I was beside the point was strong, and hard to shake. Like being thirteen again, awkward, an outsider looking at the in group. *Well, you're not thirteen. Get over it.*

I looked across the table into a bright, familiar face.

"Dave!" I said, walking over to his side of the room. I had to keep my mouth from hanging open in shock. "You look great! What . . . ?"

Dave ignored the hand I offered and enveloped me in

a lanky hug. Lightly tanned, hair tousled, he was wearing a Hawaiian shirt, a pair of shorts, and sandals. His shoulders were squared and his face almost radiant. No shuffling walk, no quivering hands. No aluminum cane.

"I found a great doctor," he said. "Different drugs, different diet. We're not even calling it remission." We grinned at each other like fools. "I feel great," he added unnecessarily. Then, before the words "multiple sclerosis" gained a foothold in our conversation, he confided his Really Big News. "I sold *Ríannon.* Lynn and I split up, and I got a sailboat. It's just a Fisher 30, doesn't point very well, but *Ariade*'s a great cruiser and a great liveaboard and I can handle her myself."

He didn't have to add that he would also be able to handle the boat if his MS came back.

"You don't have to apologize about a Fisher to me," I said. "Paul and I considered buying one when we first looked at cruising sailboats." I could still see the brochure Paul had brought home, with the photo of a man and woman drinking coffee inside the tiny pilothouse. I had wanted to be there, with them. Actually, I had wanted to *be* them. But the price was more than we thought we could afford on my teacher's salary. We built instead.

Every evening, after a day teaching junior high kids, I'd join Paul in a Visqueen shed in the middle of industrial Seattle. The smell of grinding steel and the flash of Paul's welder became as familiar as the hum of my sewing machine or the steam off my pressing board. I knew how to set a sleeve, tailor a suit. I could shape and finish fabric, so why not steel and wood?

Working on the project for the first time, it didn't take long for the image of that cozy couple to fade.

"If you're going to use those pliers, at least hold them right." I glared at Paul; the only reason I was using channel-locks was because the vice grips weren't where I'd left them the night before.

Or: "You're working too hard. There's some 36-grit paper in the box." So? With 80-grit I didn't have to worry about the belt sander getting away from me.

My turn: "I thought you said I could paint that angle iron today." Paul flipped up his welding helmet and glared at me. Wasn't it obvious that he was working as fast as he could? Could I do any better?

And so on. A million disagreements, a million decisions about fastenings and coatings, tanks and hoses, tools and wires, pumps and engines. Yet despite our arguments over when and how and how much, we were well matched: Paul the enthusiastic self-starter, I the enthusiastic finisher, both of us sure that we could do it. I grew accustomed to the weight of a drill in my hand and pliers in my tool belt. I wore out pair after pair of leather gloves, and at least one pair of boots. At a time when women wore coveralls as fashion (it was the early seventies), I wore them for their utility, and wore them to rags. My newly muscled hands grew larger. Off came the wedding ring—a hazard in construction in any case. It never went back on.

We were young—just twenty-four. And maybe because we were so young, no one stopped us or warned us that we had taken on too much, that the boat would cost ten times what we expected, and more, in both time and money.

Those older than us merely shook their heads. For months my mother would show up every Thursday evening with a hot casserole and work gloves. "I didn't think you'd ever get it done," she confided years later, "not without help." She was right; we needed the friends and family who helped us paint and haul ballast and run wire. When we launched, *Orca* was little more than a bare hull with a working engine. We had floors to walk on, unfinished plywood to keep out the rain, and a toilet. By the time we moved aboard two months later, we had added a sink with running water and a platform with a mattress for sleeping. About as romantic, my father pointed out, as living in a mailing tube.

Thinking back on all this now, I wondered at the restraint everyone exercised to not tell us we were crazy. "You know," I said, looking up at Dave, "you were smart to buy a Fisher. It took Paul and me over five years to build *Orca,* and in the end we probably spent as much money doing it ourselves."

"Is Paul here?" Dave asked.

"He's Down South," I replied, using the term Alaskans readily interpret as the Lower 48 in general, Washington State in particular. "Remodeling his mom's house."

"Lynn and I are still friends," Dave said. "She's joining me for the race. *Ariade*'s the committee boat."

"I'm on *Eagle,*" I said. "With Tim and Frank." Dave's eyebrows rose at this news, remembering that *Eagle* had won two years ago. "Don't get me wrong," I rushed to explain, though it pleased me to be associated with a winning crew. "I'm no racer. But ever since I had to drop from Joyce's crew on *Cordon Bleu,* I've wanted to try this race. Now more than ever . . ."

My voice trailed off, and Dave nodded, understanding. He too had been a friend of Joyce and Herm's, a live-aboard neighbor like Paul and me. When they'd left Juneau to sail for Mexico, it was Dave who'd been ill, and so weak he'd moved ashore, too unsteady to navigate the docks. Who would have guessed that four years later he would be so alive and Joyce would not?

For a moment neither Dave nor I spoke, and the silence seemed to comfort, inviting us to say more. But chairs were filling and the meeting was about to begin. He gave me a small smile: "Let's talk about it in Baranof."

I SCURRIED INTO A CHAIR next to Tim. My, but we were a ragged looking group. Jeans, T-shirts, a few plaid wool shirts despite the unusual warm weather. Some looked like they had just sailed into town and walked up from the docks without showering or changing clothes; their faces were stubbled and wind roughened, their hair tangled. The most startling exception was a man dressed in a white polo shirt, introduced later as a senior editor for *Sailing World* magazine. Hands down, his was the best haircut in the room.

The president of the club opened the meeting. With his clipped hair and wire-rimmed glasses, Chris had a book-ish appearance that fit with the way he called us to order. Spiral notebooks were flipped open, pencils picked up, chairs shifted forward.

Safety first, he began. Juneau might be the capital of the wealthiest state in the wealthiest nation on earth, but half-way down the channel there was nothing: no telephones, no roads, barely radio contact amid the mountains and narrow channels. Even cabins were spotty, tenuously huddled around old cannery sites. Racing through wilderness, the fleet would be on its own.

"As nice as it is here," Chris reminded us, "it can be blowing fifty in Frederick Sound." Listening, I recalled how the wind off a snowfield could change a port tack to a starboard reach in an instant, how the seas could build from flat calm to a full gale in less than twenty minutes, how quickly the dark clouds thickened. I looked around the table, feeling more like part of a team of mountain climbers than a crewmember preparing for a midsummer sailing race.

No one complained about unnecessary weight when the list of safety items was ticked off. A survival suit for each crewmember or a life raft ready to launch. A radar reflector in the rigging even though it inevitably adds wind resistance. An auxiliary engine ready to start; if an outboard, it should be mounted, not stowed away. Radio checks every four hours. No one questioned the importance of these rules.

A new ruling about safety concerned engine use. The year before, Chris's *Spindrift*, becalmed on the west side of Admiralty Island and drifting backward with the current, had come within six feet of the rocks before her anchor held.

"I came mighty close to turning on my engine," he said, pushing the bridge of his glasses. "And I probably should have, even though it would have disqualified us. I'd hate to see someone else's ego put them on a rock—we're not that kind of race." Nods all around the table; the topography above water in Southeast Alaska continues underneath, and more often than not a rock or even the shore plunges straight down, beyond the reach of most anchor lines. There had been times when Paul and I had let out all three hundred feet of chain in a futile effort to snag the bottom.

"So"—Chris took a breath and continued—"the committee has decided that auxiliary power can be used to keep a boat off the rocks if the shelf is too steep for anchoring. We already allow engine use in order to get out of the path of commercial traffic under item 4. Make the same notations in this other case." Pens and pencils moved in response.

"While we're on the subject of engines," piped up a man across from me. "Would it be okay to call commercial boats and ask them to slow down? Their wakes can do a lot of damage."

Chris turned to the committee members seated on either side of him, caught the confirmation in their faces. "I don't see why we couldn't add that," he said. "But"— a mischievous grin—"it would be improper to ask them to speed up for the racer ahead of you."

Yes, I thought, that early outsider feeling was weakening. Here was the combination of seriousness and light-heartedness I had felt cruising in Alaska and wanted to experience again in this race. And I wasn't the only one, judging from the laughter around me, and the next remark.

"We've been hearing rumors that the hot tubs aren't working," one of the Ketchikan skippers reported. "Does anyone have any information?"

"We know the store's been closed and the cabins

41

boarded up," Chris answered. "No one's charging money for the tubs."

"I heard the gangway was repaired," said one of the Juneau skippers. "But the plumbing's broken."

Murmurs. This was bad news. The layover at Warm Springs Bay was one of the rewards of this race. After a hundred miles of the first leg, everyone looked forward to a hot soak.

"If the first boats in check them out," someone said, "we should be able to get them working." Side conversations sprang up. Pipe fittings were volunteered, jury-rig repairs promised.

The problem resolved, the room grew quiet. Chris squared his shoulders and formally moved to the next item on the agenda: ratings. Pencils that had been laid aside were picked up, expressions grew serious. What Chris was about to announce marked, in a sense, the start of the race.

Ideally, all boats in a race are identical, or at least built to the same specifications; then the test is truly of teamwork and sailing skill. But in this race, like most, every boat was different. The smallest this year was a twenty-five-footer with a light outboard engine, the largest a forty-footer with a heavy diesel auxiliary. The rating numbers that we were raptly listening for were the committee's best effort to make all our boats equal. Based on a formula that factored in length, hull shape, sail area, and half a dozen other elements, the number represented the seconds per mile that would be subtracted from the boat's elapsed time. Naturally, everyone hoped for as high a rating as possible.

Chris slowly read off twelve numbers, one for each

boat. Each skipper in turn jotted his down, accepting it
with a nod, at times with the barest of frowns. Most were
sailing the same boats as last year, but a few had made
changes in ballast or sails. Tim and Frank, who had added
a new main, smiled when they heard *Eagle*'s rating: 138.

The agreeableness evaporated when the last number
was read: *Silver Girl*, 84. As if tensed for this moment, the
skippers and crews who'd raced against her in Ketchikan
immediately recoiled.

"We rated *Silver Girl* at 78 in Ketchikan," one of them
said. He was wearing short sleeves but his tan ended below
his elbows and at the T-shirt line of his open-collared shirt.
"She should have the same rating here."

"She was 84 in Tacoma," a lean young man responded
from the middle of the table, naming the Washington city
many times larger than Juneau, with a bigger racing fleet.
He spoke with the force of incontrovertible fact. His arms
were crossed, and even sitting down he looked tall. He was
obviously the owner of *Silver Girl*.

"But never rated consistently in Seattle," countered another skipper, upping the stakes. "And her last race was in
Ketchikan; that's the rating that should stand." He looked
around, appealing to everyone at the table. "Keith's boat
is *fast*."

The room erupted, voices agreeing and protesting
from every side. I and a few others were silent. This was
the first conflict to surface in this race, but the issue had
most certainly surfaced before.

"Look," Chris said, adjusting his glasses nervously.
"I move we call a private side meeting here before this

gets out of hand. One of you from each boat, all the rest outside."

Chairs pushed away from the table and voices pitched to a new excitement. I shot a questioning look at Tim as we went outside.

"What's the story here?" I asked, relieved to be away from the room and out in the brightness of the parking lot. It was easily eight o'clock but the sun was still high. It seemed to be moving horizontally above the peaks of Douglas Island, across the channel.

"The Ketchikan skippers are right," said Tim. "*Silver Girl* is fast. She's a Freres, essentially a racing machine. And the crew with him is professional." Steve, who fit that description himself, listened closely but offered no opinion. "Rumor has it that Keith is determined to win this race so he can charter it out next year." Tim was rarely critical of anyone, but his tone now was disapproving: to use this race as a way of making money just didn't seem right.

The side meeting was remarkably brief, and the conference room hushed when we returned. No one protested when Chris announced that the 84 rating would stand. No one asked for an explanation. It was written on everyone's face: The outcome of the race was now a foregone conclusion.

Then, from the opposite end of the table, came a voice I hadn't yet heard. The melodic cadence of his speech and his straight black hair and ruddy brown skin bespoke his Canadian Indian heritage. His entire manner was utterly at odds with the name of his boat.

44

"I was wondering," he asked softly, as if he were merely curious. "What's the reasoning behind *Arrogant*'s rating?"

"You won last year, George," someone volunteered. There was a little laughter, but whether in response to the joke—if it was a joke—or to our simple relief that the argument over *Silver Girl* was over, I couldn't tell.

Chris rushed to clarify, anxious to head off another conflict. "Well, we tried to get as close to a production boat as we could." *Arrogant* had been built by her original owner rather than a professional boatyard, and displayed the unlikely hailing port of Whitehorse, the landlocked Yukon Territory's only city. "And you did say you have a new sail."

"That's true," George said. There seemed to be space between every soft syllable. "But we don't know yet if the one we got fixed by the shoemaker will work." He paused for the chuckles; the problems of repairing and equipping a boat in Southeast Alaska were shared by everyone. "He told us he'd sent us a red, orange, and yellow spinnaker. The one we got today is black and white, and six feet too short." George looked around the table. His smile was perfect and beautiful.

Now we were all laughing. George's grace and humor had just reminded us what this race was all about: The real challenge might not be another boat but rather something carried on your own. The opponent to reckon with was likely to be the conditions presented by Alaska itself. And though the winner seemed obvious—*Silver Girl* certainly had all the technical advantages—a home-built boat had won once and would try again.

I caught Tim's eye, returned his relaxed smile. The high spirits that animated the meeting at the beginning had returned. When we adjourned, we carried those spirits home.

"READY TO RACE?" Paul's voice on the phone made me smile with pleasure.

"Yeah. Sort of. The weather's gorgeous, so the first leg should be pretty smooth." I'd already filled him in on the skippers' meeting. "I'm not used to *Eagle* though. I've got a lot of catching up to do." Now there was an understatement. My experience on *Orca,* I was beginning to realize, prepared me for racing about as much as driving our van prepared me for the Indy 500.

I was stretched out on Tim and Stella's hide-a-bed couch. Their voices were a burr from upstairs; now and then I heard the sound of water running, a closet door sliding. Stella wasn't joining us on the race. "No way," she'd said with a confidence I admired. Having raised her boys in a remote village and made her own way most of her life, she knew what roughing it was all about and figured she'd had enough. "A week on a cramped sailboat isn't for me." She and Tim had grinned at each other, as if in perfect agreement on this point. They'd been married a year now, and though both were in their forties they still exuded the enviable connectedness of newlyweds.

It was tempting to think of staying behind in this comfortable little house. Even if I were confined to the room I was in now I would be content, for around me, to the ceiling, were shelves so crammed with so many books that to remove one I'd have to rearrange at least two others. And between the covers of every book was a story, an adventure I could take vicariously. I could lose myself in someone else's life, with all its problems, sadnesses, and happinesses. There would be a cleanly delineated protagonist, a handful of other characters (never too many), a meaningful conflict or two (never too many of those either). There would be purpose and triumph and an ending to savor. I smiled at what Paul would say if I voiced these thoughts; for as long as we'd been together, it had been typical for me to come up with last-minute reasons not to do something.

"I wish you were here right now," I said, looking out the window across Gastineau Channel. The evening lights of downtown Juneau glittered along the water's edge. Above, the dark mass of the mountains reached up into a violet, translucent sky. "This place is beautiful—a cross between a beach cabin and a tree house." Here I was off on my own and still thinking of him, everywhere I look. *He'd love this.*

But my words were lost in Paul's. Talking long distance in Alaska often means putting up with a split-second satellite delay. When both callers talk at the same time, as we just had, the transmissions cover one another. In time you learn to sense whether the other person is done or just pausing, but we were out of practice.

"Sorry," we both said simultaneously, signals crossing again. "Go ahead," I managed to get in before Paul.

He laughed. "I was going to say it's beautiful *here.*" I pictured him stretched out in the cockpit, boats passing by on the Ship Canal. A perfect, soft Seattle evening. Night, I should say; the sun had already set there.

"How about you? All ready for Whidbey?" I asked.

"Leaving tomorrow, early." He'd spend the week ahead—his vacation—working on his mother's house. The plan was for her to move back in by the Fourth of July. About now the drywall should be going up. "Got all the supplies today. The van's loaded."

I should have stayed, I thought instantly. It was selfish for me to be here when there was so much work to do.

Paul talked on, about the doors he'd found secondhand, the hinges and weather stripping and how they'd be perfect in the entry, just as he'd hoped. He talked, light and happy, and I retreated into silence. The details that excited him seemed to pull me down. I reached back to those years together building *Orca* and tried to recover the enthusiasm I'd had then, that buoyant belief that together Paul and I could do anything. Listening to him talk about the house was like watching the distance between us expand, though somehow he got larger and I smaller, left behind. All the pleasure I'd felt when I first heard his voice turned to something else, something sad and bitter that I didn't want to acknowledge. But there it was: For the first time in our long marriage, I didn't really want to be there, helping him.

THE HOUSE HAD DISSOLVED from the bathroom outward. Paul's mom discovered the problem when she was sitting on the toilet and noticed that it jiggled. Curious, she pressed a finger on the floor next to the porcelain base and nearly went through the plywood. Rotten. She laughed when she called us on the phone: "I could just see myself on the john, crashing through to the basement."

Paul sprang into action. For him the place was more than a house. It was his childhood, his summers, his Thanksgivings and Christmases. There were photos in the family album of him as a teenager digging the septic tank and framing the roof with his father. We'd bought the place after his dad lost his job at the age of sixty and was left without a pension; we were making good money in Alaska at the time, and owning a house that we could rent back to his folks made sense.

A few years later, his father died of a heart attack: no warning except a sore back, no symptom except death. I will never forget Paul's face when he walked into my office to tell me, the bewildered look in his eyes, like a lost boy. The Juneau October was a comfort that year, rain blowing sideways, each day shorter and darker, as if the world was mourning with us. We learned, eventually, to avoid falling into the hole that was left in our lives, but it had never filled.

When his father still lived, the house seemed upright and strong, as if held together by the tall, lanky frame of its builder. A year after his death, the house looked tired and worn. By the time we resettled in Seattle, its structural weaknesses were apparent: loose mortar in the stone foundation, carpenter ants in the porch railing, rattling windows and loose jambs.

Inevitably, the bathroom floor rotted, and the timing of its discovery couldn't have been worse—just six months after I was raped. We were both doing our best to stay afloat, to hang on through the investigation and trial. I felt like I was going crazy, and for one year, and then another, it was all I could do to establish the simple routines of living. Getting on with life turned out to be far more difficult and time consuming than the cliché implied.

Paul did what repairs he could, piecemeal, until this last winter when he concluded that nothing short of a major rebuild would save the house.

I balked. I resisted. It was too expensive, too disruptive. I wanted things to be whole, not torn apart. Paul countered with the obvious. When was a better time? In twenty-five years we'd probably be living in the house ourselves; if we did nothing now it would only get worse. When would lumber be cheaper? Besides, money wasn't a problem—not really. He was doing well in architecture; I was finding plenty of work as a technical writer. He'd always talked about the changes we would make to the place someday, and here was the chance to design something his mother could enjoy now and we could enjoy later. Paul began drawing up plans, looking for contractors to do the foundation, the drywall, the framing and floors. The more he did, the happier he seemed.

All his arguments about the house made sense; I'd nod and agree and want to scream. Why was I so resistant? *Resentful*—I might as well say it outright, and as soon as I formed the word the reasons followed: Because he jumped on the project with such enthusiasm at a time when I wanted to withdraw and hold still. Because I hated the reminder of what I had been and no longer was. "I've got the energy for both of us right now," he'd say, meaning my own pace was okay, but making me feel that I would never catch up. "Someday you'll look back and be glad we did this," he'd say, and I'd recoil; the future seemed more threat than promise.

Three years, and I still had trouble moving forward, as if the violence had the gravitational pull of a planet that I would circle forever. "Recovery takes a long time," my therapist soothed, over and over. But her words couldn't erase what knife and muscle, explosive force and strangling fear, had taught me, body to body: The world is dangerous. Something horrible can happen at any time.

And the knowledge was acid.

"ARE YOU STILL THERE?" Paul asked suddenly.

"Yes!" I answered, too quickly and loudly. A long pause neither of us rushed to fill, and as if I was there with him, I watched him chew the edges of his mustache, a nervous habit as familiar to me as my own cuticle gnawing was to him. I forced my fingers away from my mouth but continued to work them against each other.

"I . . . Go on," I finally said. Even a thousand miles and an awkward connection couldn't disguise my long silence.

"Look," Paul said. "Don't worry about me or the house. There's really nothing you could do at this point." I winced at the tone in his voice. Why couldn't he just say it, that he was relieved I wasn't there, weighing him down? Why couldn't I? I closed my eyes and thought of all the times he'd held me when I cried, broken and hurt, all the early mornings he'd walked beside me when I couldn't sleep. "I know you'll be stronger someday," he'd say, and I was. But not strong enough, and if his patience was turning to exasperation now, well, shouldn't it? *He* was ready to be engaged with the world, and for him that meant fixing, building, planning for the future. The least I could do was give him some encouragement over the phone.

As he had for me, from the start, about joining this race. It had been my idea—less an idea than a reflex, actually, which struck me after Joyce's death. Tim's invitation cinched it. What was I waiting for? It surprised me, this determination that seemed part hope and part defiance. I felt as if I were flinging myself headlong into the world, grabbing something by the shoulders and shaking it: *See what I escaped? How close I came? You'll never get me!*

I sat upright in the hide-a-bed, startled, and found myself staring at a framed picture on the wall. It was a painting I'd seen many times in many places, *The Rising Wind*, but I'd never seen it so completely before: the sloping deck of a square-rigger, awash with green water; two men in the foreground, clothed in oilskins and gripping lines at the mast, as stunned as I by the mountainous seas rising beyond the bow.

A wave of unexpected helplessness—utter aloneness— washed over me. My throat tightened. "I won't be able to call you for a week, probably," I said to Paul, trying to sound composed. I gripped the headset; if I wasn't careful I'd be crying on the phone.

"I'm really glad you're doing this race." His voice was soft now, wistful; he'd heard the change in my voice. "And when you get back, I'm counting on your help." A flash, the briefest glimpse of what *he* had lost these past years: Where was I, the woman who could build a boat, chart a course, take the wheel? When we'd gone in together for counseling

Paul had explained that all he wanted was for me to be like I was before. The response—"Well, she won't be"—had crushed my spirit for days; how much worse, I wondered now, had it been for Paul?

"I love you," I blurted out, forgetting that my transmission would be swallowed in his.

"I love you." And his words—or were they mine?—echoed in the satellite delay.

THE RISING WIND

THE MORNING SKY WAS FULL of light. Not the
quiet watery light of dawn, but the bold brightness that in
lower latitudes works on me like an alarm, shouting "Wake
Up! You're late!" The sun had risen at three-thirty and
was already above the icefields. Even so, I had to struggle
against my usual morning slowness as the six of us stowed
food and gear aboard *Eagle* and cast off the mooring lines.

"Let's put you on the main winches," Tim directed me
from the wheel as we motored out of the harbor. "Mike,
you help Larry on the foredeck."

Frank and Steve were already raising the mainsail. The
metal cars securing the luff of the sail to the mast zinged up
the track. The stiff Dacron of the new white sail snapped
like a paper sack flung open. Mike and Larry raised the
genoa in a whir of line and cloth. The pawls of the port
winch sang as I cranked the handle, sheeting in.

The pull of muscle in my arms, the fresh salt in the air,
and I was fully alert now. I loved this feeling of release
from firm land to the motion of water. All the preparations
were behind, with nothing certain ahead but the race, and

that not certain at all beyond the simple description of its course: the first leg; the layover in Warm Springs Bay; the second leg; the finish. Everything else was speculation. I wasn't ready, of course; I doubted that anyone was. There was always something—more equipment, more provisions, more experience—always something to regret not having, or not having the time to do. But here we were, coming on to eight in the morning, focused on the present moment and none of us, I think, looking back. Not a word about last night's rating contest, as if so much as a quip would give *Silver Girl* even more advantage. What mattered now was us: how we placed here, at the start.

Frank turned off the engine as we joined the other boats jockeying back and forth for position in front of downtown Juneau. A north wind ruffled the water and filled all the sails. *Eagle* leaned gently to port, and without thinking we compensated by leaning to starboard.

What surprised me most was the silence. At five minutes to start, the blue flag on the committee boat—Dave's *Ariade*—was hoisted. Frank, Tim, Steve, and Larry checked their watches. In the minute between the lowering of the blue flag and the raising of the red flag, all twelve boats headed toward the imaginary starting line off Mayflower Island, on a close reach. The only sound was the flutter of sails and the whoosh of water. No one shouted or called. No gun was fired. One moment we were marking time, and the next moment we were racing.

That beginning moment almost brought us to a standstill. Suddenly we were too close to the island, had to alter course, lost all our speed jibing, the wind behind us, the wheel spinning to starboard then port, the boom sweeping across the deck, everything rattling. It was unnerving and obvious that the six of us hadn't practiced together. I fumbled like a novice, unsure where to be or which cleat or winch handle to use, unlearning as much as I was learning, my body so accustomed to sailing *Orca* that it was going all clumsy on *Eagle*.

"Other handle," Tim reminded me as I reached across the cockpit.

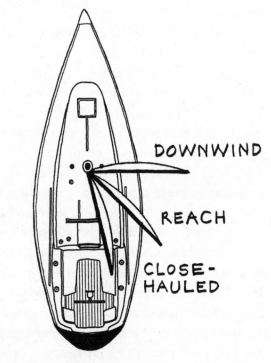

DOWNWIND

REACH

CLOSE-HAULED

BOOM / MAINSAIL
POSITIONS

"Sorry," I said, embarrassed. It was a minor mistake but there'd be others, and I was already annoyed at myself over them. *Get with it, Migael.*

For their part, Tim and Frank seemed undeterred by our ragged start. "We're still okay," Frank said, and sure enough, somehow we'd managed to place around the middle of the fleet. Lines readjusted and sails full once more, *Eagle* regained speed.

The fleet soon spread out, though the relative distances between boats remained roughly the same. With two exceptions: *Silver Girl,* already and not surprisingly pulling far ahead, and *Airloom,* rapidly falling far behind. Teak trimmed, canoe sterned, a bit tubby, nothing about *Airloom* suggested a concern for speed. The canvas dodger had been left over her open hatch instead of collapsed or removed as had been done on the other boats. Crab pots were lashed to her shrouds. A large salmon net leaned against her aft rail. She seemed to be rocking in place.

"That's the first racer I've ever seen rigged like *that,*" Steve said, looking back. The condescension in his voice silenced my own response: *Airloom* reminded me immediately of *Orca,* heavy and full keeled, roomy and reliable, a plodding workhorse among all these frisky fillies.

No point voicing these comparisons; I was on *Eagle,* not *Orca.* Racing demanded attention. We were lucky to have a north wind pushing us, and we'd better make the most of it. And in those first eight miles down the length of Gastineau Channel, we did. The slightest change of wind, the tiniest increase or decrease, and the headsail was replaced with one heavier. Or lighter. Now.

It was a routine Tim, Frank, and Larry had perfected in past races and performed so smoothly that I felt extraneous. First Frank or Tim would mention that we should change to another genoa—number 1, say.

"Number 1?" Larry would inquire softly, already moving toward the foredeck. A few strides and he'd be there, unbagging the enormous white sail, feeding the leading edge of it into the forestay so that it lay behind the sail that was already standing, full of air. He fed the sheet through its block on the fairlead track and led it back to the winches in the cockpit, where Steve and I sat, Steve more attuned than I to sheeting in at the right moment. Mike would be at the mast by then and at a word from Larry would raise the new sail. The number 1 climbed up the forestay with the slipping sound of Dacron against Dacron, visible through the standing genoa. When the new sail was up and adjusted, they'd douse the previous one, all at once, a tumble of white fabric on the deck. *Eagle* continued without a quiver, as if her sails had not been changed, but rather had grown or shrunk by some organic process.

Then the wind would rise and the number 2 had to go up and the number 1 come down. And then the wind would fall again.

With each sail change I grew more comfortable with my simple task, which was basically to wrap the sheet line clockwise around the winch, crank in and out, secure the tail at the cleat, replace the handle in the proper holster, and coil the excess line. And be ready at once to redo, or undo. I made no decisions about when and how much. I never left the port side of the cockpit, though I was twisting and

reaching, pulling in and paying out line. Would this be
all I did as we circled Admiralty Island? I didn't ask. A
hundred and ninety miles lay ahead of us—and that was
plotting without the zigzags, which are inevitable under
sail. Conditions would change.

I looked at the others. Five men. And me. Sailing all
day and through the night, living together on this tiny
floating shell for as much as a week. When Paul and I had
been on *Eagle*'s shakedown weekend cruise four years ago,
I'd liked how Tim and Frank handled close quarters and
breakdowns—normal fare on a boat. They took them in
stride. The other three crew? Larry, talking on the bow
with Mike, was obviously at ease here—no rough edges that
I could see. Mike, smiling as he followed Larry's explanations, seemed to have his dad's good nature. A quiet kid,
eager to learn. Steve? I was impressed by how quickly he
adapted to sailing *Eagle*, which, considering that he raced
his own boat professionally, I should have expected. But so
far he'd said little, smiled less, and his tanned, even features
revealed nothing. Steve seemed the least friendly, the most
businesslike. But there was the gift of the Eagle hat . . .

I touched the brim, and as happened at the skippers'
meeting last night, again I felt out of place. Here was this
group of guys, and I was tagging along. Did any of them
harbor that old superstition about women aboard bringing bad luck? I had no reason to think so—reason in fact
to think not; Larry's wife had crewed in the past, including
the year *Eagle* won. But the question still nagged. I remembered overhearing a guy once, a guy my age working
on his boat as I was on mine, out of his view. "Broads are

like that!" he'd snorted, and the men around him laughed, and though I didn't catch the context, I caught the message and felt suddenly like a kind of subspecies that didn't belong there, made fun of and erased. All of my girlness hit me then, and hit me now.

I tried to shake these feelings out of my head, toss them far out into the water. I was making too much of this, as usual. But though I tried, I couldn't imagine the guys here on *Eagle* feeling at a disadvantage in a group of women the way I always feel in a group of men—smaller, slower, less important. Always there was a hesitation, a tiny sense that my thoughts and what I've experienced in my life were less worthy, somehow. Not worth bringing up. Certainly not worth interrupting about.

If I were to mention this to the rest of the crew, they would probably look at me like I was crazy. I'd never say a word, of course. Talk about girl stuff! And it's funny that I hadn't given this my full attention until this moment. *Denial,* some would say: *After what you went through, your attack, you should expect to be anxious in a group of men.* But that wasn't it, not entirely or even mostly. My anxiety didn't feel like fear. It was complicated, more like ambivalence. And shouldn't *that* be normal for a woman who grew up with a man's name?

WHEN I WAS CURLED inside my mother's womb, in the dark wet warmth I cannot remember, my parents hoped for a boy. There were two daughters already; this time surely a boy would emerge. So they chose a boy's name, that of my mother's father: Miguel.

Miguel had died at the age of fifty-two, long before I
was born, and though I never knew him I cannot remember a time when I didn't know the story of his death: how
he'd just left a meeting at the Hispano-Americano Hall
and was headed back to his job at the printing office across
the street. How a whirlwind blew a fragment of metal
roofing from the porch, striking him on the head and killing him instantly. How just the day before he'd put fresh
flowers on the family graves for Memorial Day and said,
"I wonder who will be buried next?" The few photographs
of Miguel that remain show a face with sharp features, a
small mouth, and dark, close-set eyes. A face I see time
and again in the mirror.

The name was meant to be an honor, but growing up
it made me squirm. "Migael" marked me as different. Even
in Spanish it wasn't normal; the spelling should be "uel."
"I wanted to use the name so badly," my mother explained.
"And the 'a' feminizes it, don't you think?"

Well, no. Neither did school administrators, who assumed I was a boy and were forever assigning me to the
wrong gym class. Neither, today, do hotel clerks, visibly
taken aback when I show up as a woman. "Where did you
get that name?" I'm asked in a tone that's just the slightest bit accusing, as if I were an imposter trying to get away
with something. And I explain: the whirlwind, the metal
roofing, the interrupted life.

So it was in my childhood, explaining myself to adults.
For some perverse reason I insisted on correctness; no
sliding into Michelle or—except within the family—
shortening to Mike or some other nickname. Nor did

I pull my distinctly female middle name, Monica, into prominence. I think a part of me liked the attention, liked catching grown-ups off guard. What I didn't like was the change in their eyes when they realized I was a girl. Expecting a boy, they had prepared themselves in some way I could never have explained. Confronted with the reality, they shifted over—*down* I would have to say. But not completely, as if the fundamental nature of their error made them vulnerable, too. For me, it was an odd feeling—reckless, humbling, strangely powerful. To this day I don't understand it. But I do know that it has caused me to measure myself by what I am not as much as by what I am.

EAGLE SEEMED TO SLIDE SOUTH. Juneau steadily receded in our wake. Slowly, Marmion Island separated itself from the southeast tip of Douglas Island and grew larger.

"A foot more," Tim said as I cranked the winch for the hundredth time. A nod from Tim and I curled the smooth braided line into figure eights around the cleat.

I looked starboard toward Douglas Island and smiled. The hand-lettered sign on the isolated cabin was still there, clear and bold. Whatever the story—and there had to be a story, though no seemed to know it—the sign had been there for so long that this far end of Gastineau Channel had come to be named after it: Lucky Me.

It had been four years since I'd last read those words. Now, not yet ten in the morning, the smells rushed back: garlic, onions, olive oil, and beef. Lucky Me had always been my cue to go below and stir those sizzling ingredients, the beginnings of what Paul and I had dubbed Taku stew. A burst of memory, complete and perfect, like a meal set on a table. I could feel the heft of the Dutch oven as I lifted it from Orca's galley stove, hear the soft scraping of the wooden spoon as I stirred up the fragrances of all that had ever roasted, simmered, and stewed in that pot. We had bought it to mark our first anniversary, and with every use the hot cast iron exuded a kind of culinary history of our life together. My mouth watered and I felt a pang of longing—for the stew, for those weekend getaways with Paul, for a simple routine that now seemed like pure happiness, though it had been nothing more than inexpensive meat and ordinary vegetables cooking very slowly for a very long time.

Tim announced another sail change. Shifting position, I looked back to where we had been. Juneau was a gray smudge enfolded by the green slopes of Gastineau Peak and Mount Roberts. The channel itself seemed to have narrowed, a fjord crowded with mountains on both shores. Ahead lay a scattering of cabins that would quickly thin to one or two, then none. And then Taku Inlet and our first view, at last, of Admiralty Island.

LARRY WASN'T TAKING ANY chances. Even before we reached Marmion Island, he disappeared below. He emerged rubberized, in full rain gear: a hooded jacket, red coveralls, brown rubber boots that reached up to his knees. Ready to be doused while working the foredeck.

He grinned at the rest of us in our T-shirts, sneakers,

and jeans. "You can't trust Taku Inlet," he said, mostly to Steve, who, experienced as he was, hadn't seen first hand how thirty-plus knots of wind could hit, unannounced, off the Taku Glacier, clear skies and a warm breeze in Gastineau Channel notwithstanding.

Four channels converge on this three-mile stretch of water and at times four colliding currents and winds as well. A southerly can intensify in two directions at once, sucked northward by the narrow straw of Gastineau Channel and eastward by the glacier's vast inhale. Northerlies come off the icefields; the wind seems to gain speed as quickly as the temperature drops. In winter these are the truly danger-ous storms, whipping the water to a froth that freezes on contact with hull and rigging, spinning the anemometer at Point Bishop to one hundred knots (and more; then the anemometer blows off). Sitting at the chart table in Juneau harbor with *Orca* snugly berthed, I'd listen for the VHF radio broadcast warning of light, medium, or heavy freez-ing spray—a distinction, one Coast Guard officer joked, that's based on the size of the baseball bat needed to break the ice from the rigging. Tugs and fishing boats that had to cross the inlet at that time of year arrived in Juneau with ice sculptures of swept-back waves frozen to their bows. Some never made it. The ice became a shroud that rapidly thick-ened; top-heavy and unstable, the boats capsized. Entire crews lay entombed at the bottom of Taku Inlet, six hundred feet below.

As *Eagle* approached the sparkling blue surface, I re-membered my own worst experience of the inlet—as Tim, Frank, and Larry were no doubt remembering theirs. For me, it was a late fall afternoon, returning from deer hunting on Admiralty Island. The water had been a blue mirror when Paul and I raised anchor; by the time we reached the inlet the surface was ragged, all torn lace. *Orca* had hobby-horsed on the confused waves, her bow alternately rearing to meet the steep sea, then plunging into green water that washed over her decks, stern rising so high her propeller spun in the air. The wind speed was forty-five miles per hour and rising. Despite the jobs we were expected at in Juneau, we altered course for Taku Harbor, where we waited out the storm.

The six of us on *Eagle* stared ahead, trying to read the water. The inlet appeared to be darkened by a wind we hoped would hurry us south. No whitecaps on the surface—it couldn't be blowing even ten knots—but the blue was almost navy; somehow, the water was disturbed.

"Prepare for a sail change," Tim said, and we all sat or squatted into position, waiting. But you can't trust Taku Inlet. *Eagle* sailed into water that, though dark, was barely rippled. Instead of changing to a smaller sail, we ballooned the number 1 genoa. The temperature did drop; I reached for my sweater, Frank threw on his flannel shirt, Tim his frayed jean jacket. Larry, laughing, stripped off his rain gear.

As *Eagle* reached across the inlet, the light air filled the sails and a quiet sea gently slapped the hull. The water, milky now with silt, turned pale turquoise. To the east the cluster of rock known as the Devils Paw protruded brazenly from the icefield, marking the Canadian border. To the west the mountains of Admiralty Island rose four thousand feet straight up, creased with snow, thickly furred with green timber. Here I am, I thought, only eight miles from Juneau, surrounded already by wilderness.

Everything had a disorienting clarity. The crystal air smelled of salt and cedar. The bow wave was a mesmerizing ruffle that peeled away, dissolving into sea foam. The mountains of Admiralty Island—each rock, each tree against the sky—seemed as close as *Eagle*'s toe rail against the water. I caught myself staring, wide eyed and open mouthed, like a country hick viewing skyscrapers for the first time. I pulled off my sunglasses and rubbed my eyes, not to clear my vision but to restore it to its normal lack of clarity.

The others appeared as dazed as I was. It was something I'd loved about living here: The beauty stopped you, filled you, a surprise that never wore away.

We coasted into Stephens Passage. Blanketed and diverted by mountains on both sides, the wind softened, became fickle and elusive, striping the polished water. Propelled by a breeze we could barely feel, we eased *Eagle* along one blue stripe, then another. Our wake rolled behind us like oiled skin over muscle. The wind was a caress off our port quarter, a cool pressure behind my left ear.

On some preordained signal, Frank took the wheel. Must be noon, I thought, and sure enough, Tim was passing around sandwiches. "Stella's," he said. "And chocolate chip cookies." I knew his eyes were twinkling behind his sunglasses; when he had cruised south with Paul and me, Tim put chocolate chips in just about everything, including the pancakes.

The food tasted wonderful, and within minutes we

were talking together in a way we hadn't been up to now. Not that we had what could be called a conversation. Our talk wandered in the way that always seems to happen when traveling on water, as if the fluid substance around us has the power to dilute linear thought patterns.

"I caught my first halibut over there," I said, finishing one more cookie and pointing west across the passage. "Toward Station Point. Day like this, at anchor. Put my line in and by the time I poured myself a cup of coffee I had a fish on. It was hours before I got breakfast, they were biting so fast."

"How deep were you?" asked Mike, who had assumed his ready pose on the cabin trunk. He was dressed in shorts and T-shirt, a coiled spring, impossibly young. All of us were wearing our Eagle hats now, for shade.

"Fifty, sixty feet I think. On herring."

"Bring the main in about six inches," Tim said quietly. This was a crew of soft voices. So much, so far, for my worries about Captain Bligh personalities emerging.

I pulled the winch handle from its holster and passed it to Steve. The chromed cylinder on his side spun slowly, reflecting flashes of light. "Yeah. Better." Steve replaced the handle. Tim squinted at the knot meter; the number dropped by a tenth. "Nah, put it back out." Steve eased out the sheet, his left hand against the wraps on the cylinder, maintaining control.

"Do you have a lighter sheet?" Steve asked. He spoke in low, round tones. "She might stand a bit better." The sail was dropping at the clew from the weight of the line.

Larry moved to the bow, opened the hatch, and pulled

out two coils of what looked like clothesline. "We could switch on the next tack," he offered. "I can change the leeward line now."

A nod from Tim. When the line was within reach I threaded it through the block on the fairlead track and tied the bitter end into a figure-eight knot. By now the deck was tracked with rope.

"Just butter and a little pepper," Frank said, as if the conversation hadn't been interrupted. "No better way to cook halibut." Then, without a change in his voice, "Do you think we should try to get on the other side, Tim? They're pulling trees on us over there." Across Stephens Passage, the trees on shore seemed to be moving north behind a sailboat moving south. If we were the faster boat, those same trees would appear to be moving in the opposite direction.

"Probably a good idea," Tim agreed. "We don't want to be on this side anyway toward dark." Holkham Bay, the outlet for icebergs from two glaciers, was twenty miles south. "At this rate we may not get beyond it by midnight."

We'd been on the east side of Stephens Passage by design, not accident. Tim had figured the wind would be strongest here; according to theory, the cold air dropping off the icefields would spill out of Taku Harbor, then out of Snettisham, enough to coast us south and west with the wind off our port quarter—an easy and efficient reach. But the light air barely touched down on our side, moved instead to the west where it hit the mountains on Admiralty Island and bounced down. Boats there were being lifted with a little more speed than we were. By the time this was apparent, five miles of flat water separated us.

So we made the best of it, which meant even more attention to sailing and to every curve of the new mainsail. Steve made continuous adjustments to the luff of the sail at the mast, to the leech at the end of the boom, and along the length of the boom. He and Tim punched and pouched the smooth white Dacron, coaxing it to pillow out here, flatten there. And though they declared it an almost perfect airfoil, *Eagle* refused to respond.

"We're getting less speed out of this new sail," Frank finally said. "Let's put up the old one. At least it's predictable." He glanced from the knot meter to the sail and back again. "We should be getting another half knot. This isn't making any sense."

Despite the impatience in his voice, none of us moved. Changing the main was an unusual order, and would take some thinking through.

Steve stood in the cockpit, beside Frank at the wheel. "There's our problem," he said, scanning the mast with binoculars. "Look at the top."

Frank and Tim passed the glasses between them and instantly agreed. I could tell they were impressed by what Steve had seen: a slight bend in the mast that didn't belong there, above the spreaders and slightly to port. We all looked up.

No wonder all the adjustments had been futile. To straighten the top of the mast, port and starboard, would require adjusting the lower and upper shrouds—the web of wire that helped support the mast. Someone would have to go aloft.

Tim simply shrugged. "We'll just live with it until the layover," he said.

"That's at least twenty-four hours away." Frank sighed loudly, clearly displeased. For a moment he seemed to calculate the time and speed we'd lose adjusting the rig or changing to the old mainsail, as if working an accounting problem in his office. Then, like Tim, he shrugged, and in that shrug this first disagreement as co-captains—that I had seen, at least—dropped over the side and dissolved. "Speaking of which"—Frank's voice was upbeat again—"we might as well start the watch routine. It's after one."

The routine was simple: four hours on and four off during the day, changing to six-hour watches from 6:00 P.M. to 6:00 A.M. in order to allow for real sleep. Frank, Steve, and Mike would take the first watch; Tim, Larry, and I would take over from 6:00 P.M. until midnight. This arrangement would put two experienced racers (Frank and Steve, Tim and Larry) on each watch, with Mike and me as deck apes to help out wherever needed.

Mike and I grinned at each other, scratched our armpits, and made monkey sounds. I instantly envied his broad shoulders and bulging biceps; my upper arm was roughly as big around as his wrist. What he could do with simple strength I would have to do with leverage.

For instance, raising sail. The first third generally goes up easily, and I can hand-over-hand on a halyard almost as quickly as anyone. But as the sail is raised, the friction against the stay or sail track increases and more strength is needed. I get the strength through leverage, wrapping the line around a winch or cleat, pulling at right angles above it as I simultaneously take up the slack. The final third requires several wraps around the winch. Both my arms, along with my back and leg muscles, come into play as I crank the winch handle. It would take some practice before I knew *Eagle* well enough to do all of this rapidly.

"We'll take our break right now," Tim said, and without further prompting the three of us off watch went below. Not that we needed the rest; Tim's words were a polite way of saying that we'd get out of the way so Frank, Steve, and Mike could establish their own routine on deck.

It was a hushed, shaded world inside the cabin, like naptime in kindergarten. We took turns using the head, the rubber gaskets groaning as each of us pumped the toilet dry. Tim swung himself feet first into the quarter berth. Larry stretched out in the forward cabin. From the port berth, where I was sitting, I could hear the whisper of pages turning as they read. Both of them had brought paperback thrillers, stories to take them away from where they were. Unbelievably, I had brought nothing.

Wilderness may exhilarate and fill the spirit, but wilderness can also mean living very close to other humans. What did it matter that beyond the thin shell of *Eagle*'s hull were fathoms of water and miles of land? I was where I was: midafternoon, inside a thirty-four-foot boat for the next four hours. The two men with me had prepared for this. How was it that I had not?

It wasn't privacy I missed; I'd lived aboard too long to feel claustrophobic. What I missed, I just now realized, was purpose. On *Orca* I was always home, with chores and projects to occupy the hours, shelves of books to choose from, and—probably the most important difference— an underlying responsibility for the boat that I shared with Paul.

I thought back to Stella and Tim's library and wished I'd thought this through better. What other obvious planning had I overlooked?

"Is there something I can do ahead for dinner?" I asked, hoping to make myself useful and busy.

"It's taken care of," Larry said from the forepeak. His fuzzy head peered around the bulkhead. "We're doing all the cooking, remember?" *Right.*

I moved toward the galley anyway. "Anyone for a beer?" I asked. My own lack of resources made drinking suddenly seem like a productive activity.

"There's no beer till Baranof," Tim said gently. He didn't look up from his book. Embarrassed, I pulled a 7-Up from the icebox instead. Another one of those things I should have known without asking. No doubt part of what Frank meant when he joked about making a racer out of me yet.

I found a copy of Royce's *Sailing Illustrated* but couldn't lose myself in it. Just as well, since *Eagle*'s motion was something I wasn't used to yet and reading below deck is not the best way to adjust. I stood at the porthole above the gimbaled stove and looked toward Admiralty Island.

Nothing seemed to be occurring in real time. The sun was moving in its solstice course, high in the sky, as though it had never risen and would never set. The short shadows, the full brightness of the mountains around us, hour after hour, was as crazy-making as the long darkness of the opposite season. In the vast blue vase of Stephens Passage, time was nearly immobilizing. There were a dozen sailboats racing, but we had already spread out so far that only a few were visible in front of and behind us. The light and distance swallowed us all.

Mike thump-thumped on the foredeck, Frank and Steve mused about wind shifts and fairlead placement. I stretched out in the port berth and tried to nap.

Doing nothing—I hadn't thought through this particular aspect of racing. Standing by. Not the same as being a passenger, though I felt a little like one. What, after all, had I done so far to get *Eagle* here?

Here. And as if she had just unrolled a chart and pointed—*here*—I realized I had already made more miles into this race around Admiralty Island than Joyce.

JOYCE HAD LIVED ABOARD in Juneau longer than I, and her clothes proved it. Her brown rubber boots were broken in, her yellow rain gear scuffed and softened. A faded watch cap attempted without success to contain her dark brown curls. She was one of the few women I knew, in Alaska or anywhere, who sailed and maintained her own boat, a small sloop she'd cruised up the coast from Oregon. Walking the dock on my way home from work, I often saw her sewing or reading at her galley table. Her boyfriend's slightly larger boat, *Athena,* was rafted on the other side.

It doesn't take much to connect with liveaboard neighbors, especially in a marina like Juneau's, where everyone shares a common dock and ramp. On foot, without the armor of a car, you encounter the same people, week after week. "Good morning" and "Hello" lead easily to "Whatta you up to?" and "How's your boat?" In winter, the question becomes "Are you keeping warm?" Hoses freeze and you check with each other before turning off the water: "Do your tanks need filling?" And during those first couple of years when we didn't have permanent moorage and couldn't get a telephone, we kept our VHF marine radios on, heard each other's voices calling other boats in the harbor, could even listen in on conversations.

In all these ways we came to know Joyce and Herm as a couple. Gradually the four of us became casual friends, stopping on the dock to chat, occasionally sharing tools and recipes.

What Joyce did for a living—she was a medical technician at Juneau's only hospital—was of little importance. We rarely talked about our jobs, our families, or our feelings, as I was accustomed to with most of my women friends. Our talk was of fishing holes, anchorages, strategies for enduring the long wet winters, plans for enjoying the short (also usually wet) summers.

The first time we encountered Joyce and Herm on the water was motoring down Stephens Passage. "Orca, Orca," Herm's voice called over the VHF radio. "This is *Athena*. Switch and answer channel 68." We did, and changed course toward their sailboat. On a sea as calm and luminous as pewter, I handed Joyce what she needed, a small bag of baking soda for the carrot cake she was making. In exchange, she passed me four salmon steaks.

Another time, anchored in a small cove, Joyce showed me how to kill king crab. She rolled the spidery, nightmarish creature on to its back, held it down with her foot, and plunged a butcher knife into its belly. The long, armored legs convulsed, then fell slack. She snapped one leg off and grinned. "See?" she said. "Nothing to it." With the same directness she explained how to prepare the golden fungus called chicken of the woods, how to can sausage, how to stitch canvas. Anyone, she seemed to say, could do what she did.

I was flattered when she asked me to join her on the Admiralty Island race. *Cordon Bleu—Cordy,* she called her—had a reputation for being a fast boat and Joyce was a skillful jockey, coaxing her forward in light air, calming her down in heavy weather, just so. I would have learned so much. "Next time," I thought when I had to back out; there was no way I could handle a race with my head full of mucus and my chest full of phlegm, all of me aching with fever. *Damn.*

I watched the start from Douglas Island. Joyce had maneuvered *Cordy* into a good position before the tiller broke. She radioed Herm, made it to the dock—that woman could *sail*—and within the hour had installed a new one and was back in the race.

Most of the fleet was caught in Stephens Passage when the gale hit. *Cordy,* delayed, was in Taku Inlet—an even nastier place in a blow. Every woman on her crew got seasick. Joyce sailed into Taku Harbor to wait out the storm at anchor, but not only did the winds increase, her crew lost heart for the race.

"I would have continued," she said later, "if you'd been there."

"I would have been just as sick," I countered.

"But you would have been *there*." And I thought next time I would be.

OVER AND OVER I HEAR her speak those words. Over and over I watch her kill that huge crab. She wears a bright red jacket and her face is triumphant. Was the cancer inside her then, a tiny slumbering cell waiting its chance? I see her in the white hospital bed, the silent crab clawing at her body, devouring her soft flesh, hoarsening her voice and dulling her eyes, all her adventures contracted to that bare, colorless room.

For Joyce, there had been no next time. Yet even so I see her triumphant grin, her bright red jacket.

BY DINNERTIME THE WIND was freshening, but not enough to send spray over the bow or keep us from eating together in the cockpit. Larry served up the main dish, foil-wrapped pastries he'd made ahead, filled with ground lamb, vegetables, and a complex of savory smells: mint, cinnamon, garlic, and pepper. As we ate, mumbling our appreciation around mouthfuls, he described the recipe in detail. Food's an important part of boating: planning it, preparing it, talking about it, eating it, talking about it again. We listened with complete attention, as though Larry were telling us a story. Mugs of hot soup. Cookies for dessert.

Ten hours out from Juneau and the race had gone from

a dozen crowded, scrambling boats to this: six people in a cockpit sharing a meal, empty water all around.

Steve, Mike, and Frank went below; their next watch began at midnight and by the looks on their sun-struck, weathered faces they'd have no trouble napping until then. They closed the hatch behind them, leaving Tim, Larry, and me to handle *Eagle* alone. There was no chronometer aboard with bells to announce the time, but I knew without asking that it was six o'clock, and the unexpressed rule to relieve the watch on time was in full effect, "on time" meaning on the minute or earlier.

It's ironic how sailing doesn't free you from schedules. Racing or cruising, you pay attention to time in a way that would be considered positively obsessive on shore. The obsession goes beyond keeping track of the watch routine. High and low tides, ebb, flood, and slack—these occur at precise moments, and in inland waters such as *Eagle* was sailing were as important as wind in determining how fast and how far we would go. Frank was always checking his watch against a set of current tables his father had calculated just for this race. Like any good navigator, Tim would also know what time it was, all the time.

For this first night on *Eagle* I'd donned my full Alaska sailing gear against the cold: a turtleneck and long underwear, wool pants, sweater, cap, and fingerless gloves. Over all this warm padding, my weathered orange float-coat. Tim and Larry were dressed pretty much the same, Tim's sharp features, like mine, made more prominent by a watch cap. Larry's tight curls were apparently enough to keep his head warm.

We were now some thirty miles north of Frederick
Sound. A hundred miles away, the blue breast of the
Pacific was rising and falling; I could feel—just barely—
a low, heaving swell beneath us.

The wind turned southerly and picked up. *Eagle* picked
up with it and soon was flying, beating into the wind. The
sails quivered, the halyards pulled taut, the water blurred.
Eagle leaned to port as the knot meter hovered at 7. After
such ghosting progress all day, this was beautiful sailing
at last.

Tim, his face bright with excitement, ordered us to
sheet in the main and genoa. Close-hauled now, *Eagle*
charged ahead, rising and falling, rising and falling and
swaying and falling and rising. The two men nodded and
grinned. I tried to smile with them but, undeniably nau-
seous, I grimaced instead.

I'd felt the familiar first signs of seasickness earlier,
while changing clothes down below: a soft hammering
behind my eyes, a sour taste at the back of my mouth, a
constriction in my diaphragm. Annoyed, almost angry that
a conflict between my brain and inner ear was taking control, I'd retrieved the medication I had hoped I wouldn't
need, a scopolamine patch, and stuck it behind my ear.
That was less than an hour ago.

"I want you to know I'm feeling a little seasick," I said
to Larry and Tim; I could no longer ignore the symptoms,
which seemed to be getting worse. "I put on a patch." It
was more apology than announcement. For me there's
a kind of shame associated with seasickness, and a worry
that I might not be able to pull my own weight. Yet for

that very reason I knew it was important to admit it, even if I felt like a wimp.

"What signs should we watch for?" Larry asked, and his matter-of-fact question reminded me that his wife had often been seasick on this race. Tim listened, similarly unalarmed.

"I get a little spacey. And my reactions are a little slow. The patch makes my mouth dry—there's that awful taste. I'll be okay in a while." I licked my lips and swallowed. "I hate it when this happens."

Larry and Tim said nothing. Breathing in through my nostrils and out through my mouth, I tried to relax. I steadied my vision by looking across Stephens Passage toward the far shore. The water was deepening to maroon. The mountains were backlit by the twilight sky. Yet amidst this spectacular scenery and lively sailing, all I could think of was how I would make it through the next six hours.

Seasickness has this effect on almost everyone. With nausea comes an almost insurmountable indifference to everything around you. The whole world contracts down to your own misery. You want to crawl into bed, curl up, and moan. You want to vomit, but it rarely helps. It's not your stomach that's making you sick, but the interplay of eye, ear, brain, and muscle tension that keeps you balanced. None of this knowledge lessened the feelings one bit.

I'd long known that my body was not designed to be carried along, tossing and bouncing. As a child I'd been prone to carsickness—I was the first of my siblings to throw up in the new 1956 Ford station wagon. My first real seasickness was in my twenties, in a charter fishing boat off the Washington coast. I hadn't been able to shake the nausea, even when I hooked a salmon, though I was able to stop vomiting long enough to reel it in.

I've tried most of the remedies. My salmon fishing experience taught me that Dramamine didn't work. Pickles, vinegar, onions—they hadn't helped crossing Queen Charlotte Sound. Nor had the wristbands, with their round buttons at just the right acupressure points; I'd been so hopeful about them that I'd bought several pairs. I've heard marijuana is effective, but the side effects can be risky on a boat; being stoned is the last thing I need. Mostly, I simply make do. On *Orca,* whose motion is second nature after living aboard for twenty years, I can usually outlast the queasiness that rises in rough seas. I've learned to be careful in an ocean swell: I stay on deck, focus on the horizon, drink lots of water, and nibble on soda crackers. If at all possible, I take the wheel; steering can have a remarkably distracting effect.

Here on *Eagle,* Stephens Passage felt like open ocean, at least as far as my body was concerned. I could probably get used to the motion after a few days, but crewing a race means others depend on you. Now. *One hand for the boat and one for yourself.* It was an old saying and a true one. If anyone or anything on *Eagle* needed help, I had to be ready to give it, and that meant taking care of myself so I would be. Hence the scopolamine patch. Years ago it had pulled me through a night off the coast of Mexico.

If only the drug would kick in soon.

Everything I've read about seasickness mentions the psychological aspects, how uncertainty can create tension,

especially at the beginning of a voyage. No doubt that was
a factor; without looking in a mirror I could see the deep
vertical crease between my brows, the straight line of my
mouth. I'd brought my share of anxieties along, but better now to focus on what was right about *this* boat, *this* sea
state. *Eagle* was sound and well equipped. The skippers and
crew were experienced. The sky was clear and the barome-
ter steady. I tried to imagine what a bird would see, flying
above us: waves that felt so chaotic to me would look
ordered, the whitecaps marching with them in perfect
formation.

"Prepare to come about," Tim said, breaking into my
thoughts.

"Ready," Larry answered from the port side of the
cockpit, taking a wrap off the winch so he could quickly
release the genoa sheet.

"Ready," I echoed dully from the starboard side.
Working against the wind is just that: work. It requires
heading at an angle to the wind, first on one tack, then
on another, adjusting the sails each time, adjusting to
a different angle of heel as well when the boat leans to
leeward. No wonder it's called beating. And the zigzag of
tacking often feels like going backward. In order to reach
Frederick Sound at the south end of Admiralty Island, we
would be tacking many times during our watch, at times
toward our destination, at times away. And since this was
a race, we would tack as smoothly and efficiently as we
could manage. Although efficient was hardly what I was
feeling now.

With a "helms a-lee," Tim turned the wheel to starboard.

The genoa flogged briefly against the wire of the head-
stay as the bow passed through the eye of the wind. Larry
released the port sheet. I winched in the starboard. The
genoa and the mainsail filled.

"Smoothly done," Tim said. But in the fog of rising
nausea my efforts had felt awkward, as if I were moving
in liquid instead of air. A thick cord pulled, first tight
then slack, through my stomach, my head, all my muscles.

"So what's Paul doing tonight?" Larry asked. We'd settled into the hard cockpit seats on the windward, upward-
rising side. Tim was on the same side with us, at the wheel.

My mind shifted to another place and I managed a
weak, grateful smile; it was kind of Larry to distract me.
"Working, probably," I said, and went on to explain how
Paul was remodeling his mom's house, how he'd promised
it would be done by the Fourth of July, how at this stage
in the project I wasn't needed. Hearing myself talk, it all
sounded so smooth and settled. Not a hint of the tension
in my conversation with Paul last night. Not a hint that
the project was tearing at us.

"How about Allison?" I asked, turning the question
back to him.

"She said she was going to work on her biography."
At my quizzical look he explained. "We're trying to adopt
a baby, and one of the things the agency has us do is write
about ourselves. It's been fun, actually." His eyes, which
had been focused on the sails and the horizon, turned to
me. Deep blue, with dark lashes, all soft at the thought of
a child. "We could have a baby as early as next year."

My face relaxed a little. Thank God I didn't have an

experience of morning sickness to recall right now. Imagine feeling like *this,* day after day for a month or more on solid land. Not that adopting was easy, either. I forced myself to ignore the woozy sensation spreading upwards from my diaphragm as Larry described the hurdles he and Allison were jumping, the waiting and longing. I couldn't remember ever feeling like that about a baby. Except for—and where did this image come from all of a sudden?—my youngest brother. I had been captivated when my mother brought him home from the hospital, all wrapped up in soft flannel, tiny hands gripping my own small fingers with surprising strength. I had loved to hold him, feed him, change him. Even folding his diapers had been a treat. But by the time I was in sixth grade, all that delight was gone. Baby-sitting was a chore. And a baby was the last thing I wanted in my teens and twenties; I did everything I could short of celibacy to avoid getting pregnant. I had other plans: college, travel, a teaching career.

Paul's attitude was about the same, and marriage didn't seem to change us. Oh, there was a brief period when we talked about having children. I'd gone off the pill after being on it for over ten years, and the diaphragm was getting tiresome. It was time to make a permanent decision. We'd talk and talk about the way kids would change our lives. We both came from large families and couldn't imagine having just one. Could we raise a family on a boat? What if something happened—we lost our jobs or one of the kids was hurt or was disabled at birth or later? There were no guarantees. Where did people find the optimism to become parents? Okay, we'd say to each other, maybe we're discussing this too much. Let's decide in a month. Then we'd forget. Our maternal and paternal drives never coincided or lasted very long.

Meanwhile our nieces and nephews were born, learned to walk and talk, started kindergarten and grade school, burrowed their way into our lives and hearts, as did the children of our friends. We became aunt and uncle to dozens of kids. My teaching career gave me lots of kids to nurture and a rationale everyone accepted. Not that our parents ever put pressure on us to give them grand-children; our brothers and sisters had already done that.

So far, neither Paul nor I had any regrets. But now and then I'd think ahead and wonder: Will anyone young visit us when we're old? Will anyone take care of *Orca* when it's too much for us, the way Paul was taking care of his mom's house? Or I'd think back: If we had been parents, would we have cut loose from Seattle to try Alaska for those four years? Bought his parents' house? Stayed on our boat? Would I have walked into that laundromat that morning, into the violence that nearly killed me? And afterward, as a mother, would I have turned overprotective, smothered our children with my own fear? Even as it was I could hardly bear to look at children sometimes, thinking of what might happen to them. I watch a baby girl on the bus, her fine hair sticking straight out from her pink scalp, little fists waving. She squirms on her mother's hip as they leave, squirms from sheer joy. The bus pulls away and I watch the young woman tuck the baby into a stroller, bags and purse left unguarded on the sidewalk, the street large and noisy and the two of them so small.

In the endless twilight of Stephens Passage, I thought
of asking Larry how he and Allison had decided to have
a baby. How had they weighed the risks? But seeing his
hopeful face, I knew it was a ridiculous question. You
don't make long lists of pros and cons, then if the pros
outnumber the cons you have a baby. That's not what you
get to decide anyway—to have a baby; Larry could tell me
that. All you can do is want one. And in the wanting, all
the risks are exposed: You may be fertile or not; the preg-
nancy may go to term or not; the baby may survive or not;
the surviving children may be healthy or not. None of this,
really, is in your control.

I looked at Tim. He and Stella had married only a
year ago. Both were in their forties now—Tim was almost
fifty—and they weren't likely to start a family, though they
could.

"I'm going straight for the grandkids," Tim said, his
face almost as wistful as Larry's. For the first time it occurred to me that Stella's kids, married and parents themselves, were part of her attraction. His brothers and their
children were on the other side of the country, in Maine,
along with the rest of his family. "We get the new house
built, there'll be room for everyone." He seemed about to
say more but his hand at the wheel tensed, then his body,
then his face.

Just as quickly, I felt it too—that unmistakable sensation when a boat is on the edge of control. As helmsman,
Tim had felt it first, through pressure on the rudder. I felt
it in other ways. I could hear the soft creak as the sheet
lines strained, each strand twisting. The angle of heel on

deck steepened and my leg muscles tensed in response. The freewheeling propeller shaft, which had been humming happily, rose to a higher pitch. The wind whined over the sails and through the wire rigging. There was a little more white, I noticed, around Tim's eyes. And Larry's. Definitely around mine.

"Could you change to the number 3?" asked Tim.

Larry got up immediately and moved to the foredeck. The wind, rising to perhaps twenty knots now, called for *Eagle*'s smallest genoa. The waves had lengthened and the surface was wrinkled, like lizard skin. Crests of foam curled and broke, hissing softly. If the wind increased further, the mainsail could still be reefed down, several times.

I followed, moving sluggishly, determined to push through. My nausea was subsiding, but it was joined now by something that felt like the beginnings of fear. It had been a long time since I had worked on a heeling, pounding deck. A momentary paralysis, a flash of disbelief, then doubt. Did I know enough to help? But there was no one else.

I stood at the mast, knees flexing, ready to drop to the deck at a sudden lurch, fighting the urge to crawl back into the safety of the cockpit. From long ago I remembered: *Never let go of one strong point before grasping the next.* I fumbled for the halyard.

"Which one?" I yelled at Larry, into the wind. And he yelled back, and the line was already in my hand and everything cleared. My arms reached up and pulled down in a rhythm that was as natural as breath. My right hand wrapped the halyard around the winch, my left ratcheted the handle, then all of me cranked the sail all the way up.

86

I scrambled to the bow, and together Larry and I pulled down the number 2, lashing it to the lifelines. My body remembered, ahead of my brain, each move, each bend in the line, each piece of hardware. I knew where I could trust my footing and where I could not. I was *there*.

When we settled back into the cockpit, *Eagle* was more balanced. She was going faster, too, even though we'd reduced sail. *Because* we'd reduced sail, I should say. Too much sail puts too much pressure on rig and rudder. Heeling too far—burying the rail—might be exciting but it generally meant that the hull was dragging through the water, slowing the boat down. High excitement didn't always equal high speed.

Tim's grip on the wheel relaxed. My muscles did likewise and the last remnants of seasickness drifted away.

The wind was still strong, the waves were still cresting, but *Eagle*'s motion now was as reassuring as a cradle's. The three below had extinguished all but one red light some time ago and were rocking to sleep in their narrow berths. I tried to push the thought of such delicious rest aside.

"Am I the only one who's sleepy?" I asked, suppressing a yawn, then letting the next one stretch my jaw wide open. Our watch was barely half over and despite the long twilight I felt like I usually do on New Year's Eve: How was I going to stay awake until midnight?

"We try not to talk about it," Tim said, grinning. A yawn of his own followed.

"What we need is a story," Larry suggested. "Something scary to keep us awake."

"If we were on the other side of the passage we'd have

plenty to scare us," Tim said, indicating with his chin the entrance to Holkham Bay, eight miles to the east. The ghostly white of icebergs could barely be seen in the fading light. Those were the bergs that were easy to avoid. It was the smaller ones that were dangerous. Floating just at the surface, impossible to see in darkness, any one of them could stove in a boat, bend a propeller, snap a rudderpost.

"One of the scariest times we ever had on our boat was over there," I said. "Just outside Ford's Terror." For an instant I thought of Joyce—Herm had scattered her ashes near there a few months ago. Just as quickly I backed away from that story. *Not now.*

"You were in Ford's Terror?" Tim looked at me with disbelief. "In *Orca?*"

"Yeah." I laughed, acknowledging the craziness of it. "It was our first September in Juneau. The ice was too thick to make it into Tracy Arm, so we thought Ford's Terror would be easier. We'd been told we could make it if the tide was right." I shook my head. "We made it in all right, but we forgot to check the tides that followed. After a couple days we realized that we had one chance left to get out. It would be a month before the tides were high enough again. Jesus. And the currents in that passage really move. There's barely any slack." The inlet had been named after a man who spent one long terrifying night with his beached skiff, watching the entrance boil and swirl.

"We couldn't sleep that night," I continued, settling into my story. None of us were yawning now. "Worried we wouldn't get up in time. We were anchored way up the inlet; you've got to go that far to find anything shallow enough for anchoring, and as it was we had out three hundred feet of chain."

"What's it like in there?" Tim asked. He'd been a geologist before he turned to computer programming and was always interested in the way land was shaped.

"Magic. I've never seen any place like it, not even in Glacier Bay. Narrow, steep sided, all green-and-yellow lichen on the rocks, like gold dust. And waterfalls everywhere. Hardly any trees. I wouldn't have been surprised to see a dragon in there, or a castle. Clouds halfway down the cliffs, all misty. That was another thing we hadn't reckoned with either—fog. We sure were lucky that morning."

"Well, you got out."

"Yeah, but it seemed to take hours. We made it to the entrance—the Ford's Terror part—right at slack. And on the other side were icebergs, all traveling sideways at what looked like two knots, about what we were going. Some fairly big, half our size. Any one of them could have grounded on the shoals outside and blocked the entrance."

I took a deep breath. "We had to keep going, of course, and just hope we wouldn't be hit by one of those. There wasn't enough room in the entrance for us to turn around. It's too narrow"

Tim and Larry were silent, watching me.

"Anyway, we got out in the main inlet and it was like floating inside a margarita, all crushed ice, a yellowish gray light. We were going dead slow, me on the bow pointing to the bergs ahead, Paul on the wheel." Our faces, I recalled, had been stiff with anxiety and cold. My heart felt like it

89

stopped when a mostly submerged iceberg hit the keel near the rudder. *Orca* shuddered, and when the ice surfaced it was streaked with red bottom paint and no bigger, really, than a barrel.

"I've always wanted to go in there," said Larry. "Do some hiking and rock climbing."

"Maybe in a smaller boat," I said. "Definitely do it smarter than us. I'd make sure there was another boat in there, too, as backup. It's a canyon, and you can't get a radio signal out if you get hurt or run into trouble."

At the mention of other boats I looked around. Where were the others? Tim pointed behind, to a masthead light way over there, to another barely visible ahead. The wind, fresh and steady, continued to take us slightly southeast toward Frederick Sound. The sky deepened, lifting the veil on a million pale stars.

"It's interesting to think about getting in trouble in a place like that," Tim put in. "Not just how you'd survive but what you'd do waiting for help to show up."

"Play," said Larry. "That's one of the most important things. There were these people on Prince of Wales Island I read about, two groups that washed ashore after a storm, and the big difference between them wasn't food or shelter but how they spent their free time. The group that knew how to play were in better shape afterward."

"I remember hearing about that too," I said. A Coast Guard survival film had shown a group sitting around playing guessing games, checkers with rocks. "What I'd like, if we got marooned, is someone with us who's memorized poetry."

"Well you're in luck," Larry said. "I happen to know 'The Cremation of Sam McGee.'" He cleared his throat and without any prompting recited the entire poem. All fifteen verses. Only once or twice did he pause to recall a phrase. Now and then we adjusted sheets to make as much speed as we could. Tim made subtle changes to our heading. But our minds were on Lake Labarge, hunting for gold in the frozen Yukon, longing for Tennessee. And finally, gratefully, warming our souls in the roaring crematorium fire.

"Prepare to come about," said Tim, breaking the silence that followed Larry's astonishing recitation. We went through the paces of tacking and settled ourselves on the high side of the cockpit.

"That's a hard act to follow," I said, wiping my nose; it always dripped in the cold. "About all I can think of right now to offer is 'The Teddy Bears' Picnic.'" After what Larry had just done—he was definitely on my shipwreck list—singing a simple children's song would be easy.

"Let's hear it."

I cleared my throat. "When you go into the woods today," I began, softly at first, then clearly, happily: "You better go in disguise." I paused, half expecting to be stopped, but both Tim and Larry were looking at me with encouragement. I picked up the tune in earnest and sang on, of bears being watched unaware, having fun, of good bears who were gathered by their parents and tucked into bed after playing games and eating wonderful things. Every bear that ever there was.

Tim and Larry joined in the refrain and our ragged

voices trailed off the stern with *Eagle*'s wake, west with the wind to Admiralty Island. Where real bears lived—one per square mile, the highest density of bears in the world.

A BEAR TAUGHT ME what wilderness was, and I didn't have to see it.

Paul and I had been hiking up a stream on Admiralty Island. At first we walked on rocks, but eventually we branched off to a trail that led into thicker brush. Soon we were in a green tunnel almost as wide as my arm span. The path was pounded smooth, the air thick and musky. Before I understood the reason, all the tiny hairs on my body tingled: *This isn't our trail.*

"I want to go back," I said.

Paul turned to me. "Good idea." He had felt it too. Something up ahead, or off to the side, watching. Uninterested or annoyed, content or angry, but if we crossed its path *it* would be in control.

That was the first time I knew, completely and viscerally, that I was a prey species. In those woods I was reacting on instinct, quicker than thought, in ways I can explain in hindsight but which at the time simply took over. My heart accelerated and my surface blood vessels constricted, conserving my body heat, nourishing my muscles and brain for danger. Adrenaline flooded through me, slowing time and pitching my senses so high that I remember, to this day, each separate leaf and twig. Walking back, I had to make an effort not to run.

Later that evening, Paul and I did see a brown bear on the beach; even from the safety of *Orca* it was humbling. So was finding a bear track in the sand and comparing it to the imprint of my own booted foot inside it. Or motoring along in Glacier Bay and noting, with surprise, that the brown bear foraging on shore, turning over rocks, eating limpets and licking salt, was keeping up with us at seven knots.

To see a bear in the wild—it was as if Nature was revealing her living heart. This wasn't the benign Nature Thoreau found on Walden Pond or the affirming land-scape of the Romantic poets I'd read in college. Or, for that matter, the peaceable kingdom of my generation's back-to-the-land hippies. This Nature had more in common with what primitive people experienced, full of dangerous spirits that had to be respected and appeased. In bear country, I was that person, responding in primal ways. There was no point reducing bears to a symbol of the wild in my own civilized world; they were living creatures that breathed, foraged, killed, ate, slept, reproduced. And defecated—did they ever—in the middle of a trail, leaving a pile that, by its warmth, was often all that a bear revealed of its proximity, and its probable awareness of me.

From the deck of *Eagle*, in the middle of Stephens Passage, the thought of a bear was just that—an abstract thought. We could linger on their playfulness, their teddy-bear side, bears as we've seen them in circuses or zoos. But were we to head toward shore and set foot on Admiralty Island, we'd drop the fantasy and pool together all that we knew about bears—*real* bears. Not to titillate ourselves or be morbid; not even to make ourselves feel brave. We'd remind ourselves of the reality of bears because that was the best way to survive.

93

On every level, their reality is incredible. Take the obvious: size, speed, and appetite. Most bears stand as big as a pony, an animal they can easily outrun in thick terrain and almost keep up with on the straightaway. They move though blueberry bushes like a combine. They eat everything: grass, skunk cabbage, soiled diapers, long-dead salmon carcasses. When their favorite food is plentiful, they become gourmets, eating only the most delectable part of the salmon, the liver and heart of a fawn. When food is scarce (or perhaps when they simply feel lazy) they move boldly into human habitations, right into a hunter's camp to snag a backpack, right onto the back porch to get to a garbage can. Once, in downtown Juneau, right up to the glass doors of the supermarket.

Those rounded fuzzy ears give them a lovable look from a distance, but what matters up close are the teeth and claws they use for killing as well as eating. Bears have a capacity for aggression that no one understands and that's hard to accept. The idea that a female with cubs would kill to defend them fits our sense of how the natural world should be; that an adult bear—usually male, sometimes female—would kill a smaller or younger member of its own species does not. Few mammals, other than humans, do so. The best guess researchers offer is that, since bears don't depend on each other (mating and raising cubs being the exceptions), they simply never evolved to be social, at least not in the way we understand the term. It's not that they're antisocial. For the most part they get along when a food source brings them together. Perhaps their overtly aggressive behavior is a quirk.

In Tlingit legend bears are related to us, and it's easy
to see why. They whine when attacked. They make tears.
They can stand on two legs. When skinned, the carcass
looks like a human corpse.

When a human and a bear encounter one another, the
result is usually peaceful. Rarely—very rarely—is it violent.
Everyone in Alaska talks about the violent stories. One of
the most famous is about the Forest Service employee who
watched and felt her own arm being eaten by a black bear;
Tim and Larry both remembered when that happened.
On our second cruise to Glacier Bay, Paul and I had been
warned away from North Sandy Cove, where a hiker
had been attacked and devoured down to his boots by a
brown bear. The rangers knew it was a brown bear (for
some reason they're never called grizzlies in Alaska) from
the photographs in the camera found at the camp, which
showed the animal as it steadily approached. A man Tim
and I taught at the university in Juneau bore the scars of a
bear attack that had left him blind. The bear had taken his
head into its mouth and bitten down—a grisly signature.

With stories like this, it's easy to get the impression
that every bear is unpredictable and dangerous. But most
bears are neither. Those who watch bears in areas where
salmon runs bring them together describe their individual
personalities as being remarkably predictable, season after
season. But the predictability breaks down when you com-
pare one bear to another. A few are predictably aggressive,
most are predictably not; again, like humans. What this
means when we come upon a bear is that nine times out of
ten—so the popular phrase goes—the bear leaves quickly,

as though human contact was repellant. The trouble is that these odds are no comfort if you happen to run into the tenth bear.

So the advice on how to avoid a bear attack is plentiful and enthusiastically shared; the three of us on *Eagle* could have practically recited it. When hiking, make noise on the trail (that was my inspiration for learning all the verses to "The Teddy Bears' Picnic"). Don't hike if you're menstruating. Don't wear sunblock or lotions that make you smell like something to eat. Don't store food in your tent. Be extra cautious if you see a cub; even an eight-hundred-pound male keeps his distance from a mother bear. If approached by a bear, don't ever turn and run; it's sure to trigger a chase, which you can't win. Back away slowly instead, and drop a cap or some other object to give the bear a distraction. Avert your eyes; bears see a direct stare as confrontation. The bear researchers I knew in Juneau had adopted this deferential behavior so thoroughly that in human company they seemed almost unfriendly. Talking can help; the Tlingits, who encountered bears for thousands of years without the backup of firearms, respectfully addressed them as Grandfather or Grandmother, explaining to the animal who they were and what they were doing.

If the bear attacks and is on you, play dead; your final hope is that the animal will lose interest. This is especially important if it's a brown bear; struggling is likely to excite it, and it won't do you any good anyway against five hundred pounds or more of muscle and fur, teeth that can crush bone, and claws that can puncture steel cans. Your best weapon is your brain, but if you do carry a firearm make it a rifle with enough power to penetrate forty-two inches of wet phone books—a detail described with particular gusto at a Forest Service talk Paul and I attended in Juneau. And since most charges are bluffs, you've got to be cool headed and skilled enough with that rifle to wait until the very last moment before shooting.

Native Alaskans had no taboo against killing a bear, but the rituals around the kill were important. An Admiralty Island Tlingit described how the animal should be skinned, paws up, to help it stamp the clouds on its way to the spirit world. Modern hunting regulations in Alaska also acknowledge the bear's special place, if only as a resource that attracts tourists. In some regions, Alaska residents may take only one brown bear every four years. Nonresident hunters must hire a licensed guide or be accompanied by an Alaska resident who is in the second degree of kindred. Hunters aren't required to purify themselves first, as the Tlingits did—some still do—but the regulations prescribe extensive rituals of salvage, transport, and possession. Every bear killed must be examined by a Fish and Game officer. When a bear is killed in self-defense, that killing must be reported, the head and hide surrendered, a thorough investigation made. It is as if a human has died.

ALL THESE RULES AND TRADITIONS, all this advice. But the most important perspective I learned was from Carl. About the same time the black bears could be seen on the slopes of Mount Juneau high above the harbor, Carl would appear on the dock, as much an indicator of spring as they were.

"Yup, gotta fix her up," he'd say loudly of his boat, to himself if no one was around. I could hear him from inside *Orca*. "Got a full season of hunters this year." As if that was unusual. Carl was a sought-after bear guide, and the hunters who paid $10,000 a week for the privilege of his experience came from all over the world.

Carl wasn't a particularly big man, but his gestures were, and his voice and spirit. Utterly at home in the world, Carl walked the same way in any weather, never hunkered against the wind or rain, even when it came at him sideways. And he was always dressed the same way too, in khaki or gray-green, as though he'd grown his clothing the way an animal grows its coat.

Heron, his overbuilt wooden trawler, was as unadorned and direct as Carl. Gray hull, gray cabin, gray decks, the simplest of instruments, nearly Spartan accommodations. It was a tribute to Carl's skill as a bear guide that hunters who could afford greater luxury chose him above others. On some trips, when he was hired by photographers or when the hunters were bad shots, no bear were killed. But most often he'd return to the harbor, *Heron*'s foredeck draped with bearskins, heads attached.

"Beautiful animals," Carl would say, as if the dead remains on his deck had spirits. "And *smart*. But people get too carried away about bear attacks, spend too much energy planning for one. A guy's safer walking on Admiralty Island at midnight than he is in broad daylight in downtown Seattle." He didn't mean to sound tough and could as easily have referred to Franklin Street in downtown Juneau. Behind that statement was a harsh reality he never

spoke of on the dock: a son who'd been murdered on a
fishing trawler by a crewman. The murderer was incarcer-
ated only three miles away, at the prison in Lemon Creek.

There was the great irony, and Carl was the only one I
knew to ever mention it directly. All the survival talk that
centers around unlikely encounters with dangerous bears,
when the greatest chance of violence is at the hands of another human being. Looking back now, I saw that violence
myself. There was the pair of fishermen in Ketchikan,
friendly enough at first, who took after each other with gaff
hooks. There was the young man living in a derelict scow in
Juneau who was suspected of killing his girlfriend; he walked
the dock one night carrying a hatchet, muttering about "getting even" with a "friend." There was the "respectable" liveaboard who, in a rage, attempted to strangle our friend's cat.

The explanations were always the same: too much al-
cohol or too many drugs, too much isolation or too much
crowding. But I wonder now if these men were simply the
equivalent of the tenth bear.

I SAW LOTS OF BEARS in Alaska, always at a comfortable distance, always with that rush of awe and tingle of
fear. It's likely that even more bears saw me. Hiking, there
was always the risk of an encounter, but the risk was exhila-
rating; it made the wilderness *wild*. I was alert, I was prepared, I sang right out loud and off key to keep the bears
away while I picked blueberries in the woods. That had
been me—not fearless or reckless but confidant and relaxed.

Then I encountered the tenth bear Carl had warned
of, in Seattle, in broad daylight. I felt what I'd felt on that

long-ago trail, magnified a thousand times by a human body forcing itself over mine and into mine, strangling hands stopping my very breath. And remembering all the advice, knowing as completely as I would have known in the grip of a bear attack that physical resistance was useless, I went limp. I played dead.

How different if it had been a bear. I would have been a hero, my story sought out and eagerly listened to. Pitted against such a glorious foe, I would have acquired some of the bear's glory. But it was an ordinary-looking man; no claws, no fangs, no roar to announce his brutality. A rapist—caged for now—and an ordinary, everyday crime.

Pitted instead against such a man such as that, is it any wonder I feel so little triumph in my survival?

EAGLE RACED OVER the trackless sea, parting the waves. Spray glowed against the running lights, green on the starboard side, red on the port. Beneath us were living creatures, unseen. Against us was the wind. The sky was deep violet and scattered with stars—it would get no darker on this solstice night.

Our watch almost over, the three of us had been silent for some time, speaking only when we tacked, moving nothing but the rudder and the sails.

AFTERNOON: WE WERE DOWN to our T-shirts again and *Eagle* wore her lightest genoa. Sunblock was much in demand. I'd started with protection factor 8 but was now squeezing out and liberally applying 20. The bill of the cotton baseball hat Steve had given me was pulled down to my eyebrows. I could have used flaps around the bottom, like a French Foreign Legion hat; headgear designed for the Sahara made a strange sense here on the glassy expanse of Frederick Sound. The sun's reflection in the water was as blinding as welding flash.

This was our second watch of what was turning into a very long day. I'd woken that morning to the clang of halyards against the aluminum mast, and when the three of us took over in the cockpit Tim had teased Frank, Mike, and Steve about losing "our" wind. That was almost twelve hours ago, and through alternating four-hour watches we'd coaxed *Eagle* little more than twelve miles, spending every one of those hours in unrelenting attention to the sails, the wheel, all the instruments.

There was no sensation of racing. The competition had diminished to tiny white triangles here and there, and they seemed motionless. The calm stretched as far as I could see. Where had last night's wind gone? Periodically, Tim would call the committee boat to announce our location and listen as other skippers announced theirs; from this information he could extrapolate our position in relation to them. For me, it was all quickly forgotten. I did my best to be part of the endless discussions about sailing in such light air (should we cup the leech more? ease the luff?), but more and more I depended on Tim and Larry to supply the energy to keep racing. My mind, as becalmed as *Eagle*, wandered easily from the task of moving as fast as possible when "fast" was very nearly standing still.

Forward movement seems to require conflict: in a powerboat, the controlled explosion of fuel inside an engine; in a sailboat, the force of moving air against the sails. Kayaks, canoes, and rowboats depend on the strain of muscles and bones. Something must push against something else or nothing moves. In our case, we had only the barest breeze to work with, and it was more of a challenge than last night's southerly. More than a full gale, for then the adrenaline our bodies produce on instinct would make us pay attention, be clever and strong. Biology helps us to be heroic. When what we need to work against is tedium, or barely perceptible changes in wind or current, we must dredge the will from down inside to perform well.

I squinted up at the genoa. It seemed to be filled more with heat and light than with wind. I spat into the sea and the tiny bubbles of saliva slowly coasted away. Against Admiralty Island, toward Herring Bay, was a pod of humpback whales, the distant plumes of their breath like geysers. Now and then they dove, their flukes disappearing into the water without a splash. I held my breath, as if descending with them.

"Let's bring the number 1 across." Tim's voice brought me abruptly to the surface. "I think we might get a lift from shore."

We had been gradually moving toward Admiralty Island on the chance that cool air dropping off the mountains would create enough wind to push us south, where we needed to go. Almost fifteen miles of water, so calm it seemed molten, separated us from Yasha Island, our next destination. From there—we scarcely talked about this yet, it seemed so remote—we would reach northwest another ten miles across Chatham Strait to the finish line of Warm Springs Bay.

Larry nodded, more to himself than to Tim, and moved to the bow. He crouched down to keep his weight low, every step deliberate and soft. I released the sheet from the starboard winch, checked that the line was clear, then moved with similar caution to the port side. The genoa swished like taffeta as Larry gently pulled it to the other side of the bow. I wrapped the sheet around the port winch, though I could have pulled it in with one hand. The main boom shifted to port, barely. Tim turned the wheel, ever so slightly.

We held still and watched the genoa fill. A long pause, and then the digits on the knot meter changed: .4, then .5, then it held at .6. Tim's hunch had been right. Never mind that our speed was less than a knot. Despite appearances, we weren't drifting, and every bit of progress we had made so far today we had managed to retain.

The success of our maneuver made us suddenly optimistic and talkative. If we could maintain this course and speed, we just might make half the distance to Yasha Island by nightfall. Perhaps the wind would pick up toward dusk—surely Frederick Sound was too nasty to behave peacefully for so long. We fell silent again; bad luck to tease the elements. A shift of weather systems in the Pacific and we could as easily be scrambling to slow down, beating against a southerly gale that pushed everything before it toward the rocks off Admiralty Island. Better to accept what wind we had.

Laid open as it was to the ocean, exposed to whatever happened there, Frederick Sound had a way of humbling the overconfident, reminding us even in this calm that we're all on the food chain. Those humpback whales that seemed to be languidly basking in the afternoon sun? Most likely they were working, not resting or playing, sifting enormous mouthfuls of silver herring from the sea. On a day like this the herring would be deep and the whales would dive in a circle to bring them up in nets made from the bubbles of their breath. If salmon follow the herring, an eagle—sometimes several—will be there, as though alerted by a special bulletin. They hit the water feet first, white-feathered legs and yellow talons spread wide, and crawl back up into the air with their wings.

This isn't sport but a matter of survival: for the herring, for the whale, for the salmon, and the eagle. If the salmon is large, it will keep swimming, the eagle's talons deep in its back muscles. The eagle, whose grip operates on much the same principle as a pair of ice tongs, cannot release the fish and may be drowned by it. I once watched just such a miscalculation: an eagle, weighted down by its catch, swimming a splashy breaststroke for over a hundred yards, its wings and head just above the surface of the water. By the time it reached the beach, the eagle was too exhausted to do much more than contain the thrashing fish among the rocks, the bleeding fish too exhausted to make it back to deep water. Soon a half dozen ravens hurled themselves gracelessly into the fray. Shameless opportunists, they weren't intimidated in the least by the eagle, which they noisily chased off. Before the fish stopped moving it was being eaten. The ravens tore living flesh from the salmon and flew or hopped away, tried to swallow what they'd robbed before another raven robbed them. Gulls slipped in where they could, adding their cries to the ruckus. For an hour the eagle stood off. The tide retreated. Then, ignoring all protests, the eagle returned, lifted the now-manageable salmon carcass into the sky, and flew into the forested mountains.

So much effort simply to eat. By comparison, we aboard *Eagle* were privileged princes and a princess, protected in a capsule of plastic and Dacron, fed with a regularity the creatures around us would probably love to get used to. Cars and an airplane and a boat had brought me here to Frederick Sound, not my own legs, fins, or wings. What right did I have to declare the day peaceful or the wind too calm?

OUR WATCH WAS ALMOST over, and soon the others would be topside to take our places. We would have a meal and a nap before we resumed our watch at midnight, as they had yesterday evening. I wasn't tired yet—it was only around five in the afternoon—but the watch routine had enveloped me in its own rhythm and I knew I would be able to sleep on schedule. During our four hours below I'd kept myself firmly awake, first by serving lunch with Tim and Larry and cleaning up the dishes, then by carefully repacking my duffle bag so the warm clothes I'd need for our midnight watch would be handy—my seasickness seemed to have been cured by the scopolamine patch, but I didn't want to risk a relapse by searching through my bag later. And lastly, most delightfully, I'd stayed awake by paging through the already well-thumbed *Sailing Illustrated*. Like a traveler in a foreign land who reads with a translating dictionary, I'd eagerly reviewed the sections on rigging tension, sail trim, and steering balance, eventually losing myself in the glossary. Wonderful words! I found favorites under every letter of the alphabet: baggy-wrinkle; cutwater; deadrise. All I could think of right now for the letter A was ash breeze, a wind so calm a sailboat was forced to use its wooden oars.

Frank poked his head up through the hatch, yawning and blinking in the brightness. He looked all around, making a 360-degree survey. In the four hours since he'd been on deck, we had made perhaps four miles. The scenery had hardly changed.

"Is this it?" he asked, and our sense of accomplishment dissolved. But only a little; we'd had the same thought that morning when we saw that he, Steve, and Mike hadn't yet cleared the Brothers Islands.

Frank's observation wasn't surprising, but the suggestion he made, almost in the next breath, was. "I've been thinking," he said. "Let's drop from this leg of the race."

Tim, Larry, and I turned in disbelief. *Quit? Now?*

"Look," Frank continued, "we've barely moved against the shore. We"—meaning his watch—"won't be able to do any better than you guys." Frank had obviously been thinking about this for a while. "We've still got over twenty miles before we reach Baranof. At this rate it'll be tomorrow evening before we get there." Wouldn't conditions change before then? Well, they hadn't for the last twelve hours.

Every reason Frank gave made sense, and he hadn't

even mentioned the strong currents and unmarked rocks around Yasha Island. But Tim wasn't nodding. Larry and I said nothing, of course; this wasn't our discussion or our decision to make.

"We've already placed last in this first leg," Frank offered, speaking directly to Tim. "We can still race the second after tuning the rig; we'll need time at the dock for that." No one could be sure about the first statement, but the second was certainly true. "Besides," Frank added, "we need time to play."

Play? Frank was talking the way Paul and I talk when we lose the wind or it gets too rough or too late; we take down the sails and head for the nearest anchorage. The thought of a cozy mooring and a hot soak in the tubs at Baranof was enticing, but it was Frank who had said yesterday, when my attention wandered, that I should learn to think like a racer.

By now Steve was on deck, and somehow I wasn't surprised when he spoke up. "Look, while you guys discuss this, why don't the rest of us clean up the foredeck?" He called down the hatch and Mike emerged, shrugging and smiling slightly.

Frank and Tim went below. In the silence they left behind, the four of us sorted out the sails that were piled and billowed port and starboard from endless changes. We pulled the white Dacron along *Eagle*'s deck, loosely folded each sail from the middle, and stuffed it into its bag so that the head, clew, and tack were on top, ready to be snapped onto halyard, stay, and sheet. We said nothing about the discussion going on beneath our feet. If Steve had talked it over already with Frank—and I felt certain he had—he never gave a sign. There was a slowness in all our motions and in our talk, a kind of reluctance, like a sailboat caught in irons, unable to fall off to starboard or port, unable to go forward against the wind either way, on the verge of going backward. Yet *Eagle,* unattended, stayed on her barely perceptible course, main and genoa full, still racing.

Tim was out the hatch ahead of Frank. "Drop the sails," he said—all he had to say to announce the decision. There was a tightness around his mouth, a resignation in his eyes. His gestures were a little stiff.

Frank moved toward the engine compartment, and I winced at the noise that would soon erupt from there.

"Before turning on the engine," I asked, on impulse, "could we drift, do you think, through dinner?" It was the first time I'd interrupted anything, and I felt a little foolish, especially since everyone was now looking at me, eyebrows raised. For a moment I considered backing down or explaining the obvious, that once the engine was on, this leg of the race was over, that I wanted to postpone that moment, if only for a little while. Then everyone's face relaxed—even Tim's—and Frank sat back in the cockpit in a way that said, *Yeah. Good idea.*

"And while we're bending rules," put in Larry, with the barest of smiles, "let's break the one about waiting until Baranof to have a beer."

WE WEREN'T GIVING UP entirely, we told each other through the rest of the evening. There was still the second leg of the race. *Eagle* might make a good showing yet.

But *quitting*—at all. It was the last thing I'd expected.
I'd been steeling myself for violent weather, equipment
breakdowns, crew conflict. That we might be stopped like
this had never occurred to me. Sure, Joyce had quit the
first leg, too, the entire race, in fact, but for the opposite
reasons—too much wind, too much seasickness. I couldn't
imagine her quitting because it was too *calm,* no matter
how frustrated or bored she got.

Disappointment stirred, and small, mutinous thoughts
surprised me. What is a race if not a commitment by all
participants to complete it, even—perhaps especially—
when completing means losing? No matter how we
phrased it, we were quitters; worse than losers, for turning on the engine disqualified us completely from this leg,
putting us behind even *last* place. What would the other
crews say? "We'll take our lumps," Frank said, and while I
admired how he could put his ego aside, that wasn't what
I worried about. This decision was bound to affect the
other boats. If everyone but the winner quits, can there be
a real win?

I never voiced these questions—it wasn't my place
and it wasn't my boat. Nor, if they had them, did anyone
else voice theirs. Boats aren't democracies; it was our job
to accept what the captains decided. And it went without
saying that when we met up with the other boats at Warm
Springs Bay we would all support *Eagle*'s decision.

I tried to imagine how Tim and Frank had come to
their decision and immediately thought of all the disagreements Paul and I have on *Orca.* He'll want to run in fog and
I won't. I'll want to head out and he'll want to wait. I'll

want the sails up and he'll want to motor. Anchoring itself can set off an argument.

"We're hooked," Paul says. We're both watching the chain go taut as the anchor bites. *Orca* swings around.

I frown. "That boat there seems a little close." I point to a trawler that seems to be swinging toward us on its anchor line.

"So where's a better spot?" Paul's voice is testy and I bristle with resentment that he's taking my opinion as criticism. I have the right to speak up. He does have a point, though, about the anchorage. There is no better spot.

I shrug and admit that we're probably fine where we are. Neither of us wants to crank up 150 feet of chain by hand and reset the anchor. Neither of us wants to argue, either. We pick a tree and a couple points on shore, mentally triangulating our position, and watch in silence as *Orca* swings, bow to the northeast, like the boats around us.

"Let's make sure," Paul finally says, and backs down, full throttle toward the trawler. I nod, glad that he heard the worry in my voice, though he didn't say so. *Orca* holds firmly; if not, we re-anchor, grumbling but fully aware that we'll both sleep better for the extra effort.

As for the resentment, the testiness, the near argument— we let those feelings go, too distracted by stowing gear and settling in for the night, too safely anchored to dissect how we got there.

EAGLE'S ENGINE BROKE the stillness. There would be no midnight watch, so I stayed on deck until the sun was well behind the mountains and the sea turned silver.

I wondered at the feeling that spread over me as we motored toward Baranof. The disappointment was still there, maybe a tiny resentment, but both of them together weren't as strong as my secret, perverse relief. No test tonight of how well I could stand watch from midnight to six in the morning. No wondering about the wind or what sails to use. No doubts about how we would place in this leg: We wouldn't, at all. Instead the dependable engine would move us along at a predictable five knots. *Safe and sure,* and as soon as I thought the words I realized why I was so relieved. Safe and sure had become my habit. That and letting others decide. Risk nothing, lose nothing.

I knew this was an important thing to recognize, and a shameful thing too. In joining this crew I'd given Tim and Frank the assurance that I would try to do whatever they asked. Okay. They were quitting the first leg—their decision, not mine—and though I was confused by it at first, only an hour later I was simply relieved. Off the hook. Relaxed, to be honest.

Maybe I was taking it all too seriously. What, if anything, were the men around me saying to themselves? That it was only a game? That there was always next time? They weren't saying anything to me, that was for sure, just as I would never, ever admit my feelings to them. But having been told to retreat and feeling glad to do it, would I—would any of us—as readily advance?

Repairs

I WAS BELOW, on the edge of sleep, when *Eagle* motored into Warm Springs Bay in the gloom that passed for night. The engine shifted into idle, then fell silent. I heard the thumps of feet above me, and Frank's voice as he directed Steve and Mike through the geometry of mooring: Make the bow line fast here. Take up the slack there. Let's run a spring-line from here to there. A few minutes later, the sound of the hatch sliding closed, the clunk of shoes, the zip of jackets.

The next time I opened my eyes it was to the white light of morning. *Eagle* was strangely still. Inside my sleeping bag, I felt over-warm, greasy and sticky. My scalp itched. *Boy, do I need a bath,* I thought, yawning and rubbing my hands across my face, around my eye sockets. I looked across the cabin; in the berth on the other side of the table, not four feet away, Steve looked back at me. I froze.

"Yes," he mouthed. "They're working."

The baths. He's talking about the baths. In my waking I'd forgotten that I wasn't alone in the main cabin. I caught my breath and nodded. Had he seen me flinch? But he was

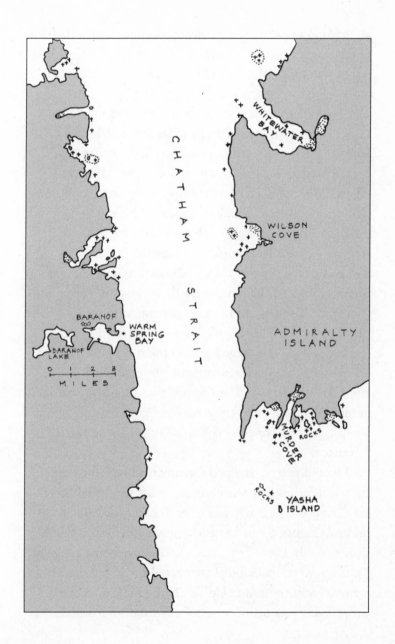

113

already out of his sleeping bag and rummaging through his duffle, as if my nod had been an offer to go with him. Why not? I was wide awake, and Steve didn't know where the baths were.

I pulled on my jeans and sweatshirt, grabbed clean underwear and a T-shirt, soap and a towel. Without a word the two of us tiptoed out the hatch, across *Eagle's* cockpit and across the boat we were rafted to, *Casa Mía*. Then briskly, as if we were late for an important appointment, we walked up the dock toward the ramp.

We needn't have rushed. No one else was around. It was earlier than I'd thought, no later than six. The bay was a mirror of the sky, deep lapis. The mountains, impossibly green, embraced the water with their enormous arms and shoulders. East, beyond the bay's narrow entrance, Chatham Strait glittered. The tide was out; ravens, shiny as patent leather, walked bowlegged among the rocks and seaweed. All business, they investigated the pungent muck with their beaks and claws, then tipped their heads skyward to swallow. They ignored the crows and gulls feasting beside them. Squabbles over food would come later, as the sea advanced.

I wouldn't have guessed that my readiness for a hot bath would coincide with Steve's, of all people. Although we'd lived within thirty feet of each other for two days and two nights, we hadn't exchanged more than a few dozen words. Part of that was the result of being assigned to different watches, but I suspected the main reason was his taciturn nature. Unlike Tim, Frank, and Larry, Steve didn't volunteer personal information. I still didn't

know what he did for a living; Tim thought it was something to do with investments. He was married, I knew,
to Frank's sister, but I had no idea if they had any kids or
where they lived in Seattle. Nothing about him invited
such questions. Steve had the crisp handsomeness of a
man for whom appearances mattered, and of the six of
us—including Mike, so young and, around me at least, so
shy—he seemed the most reserved. I hadn't yet heard him
really laugh or joke. It was as though racing was something
that deserved all his attention and everything else—the
personalities, the scenery, the food—was of secondary
importance. Even now, heading purposefully up the ramp,
he seemed contained.

The wood-frame buildings that crowded around the
boardwalk at the top of the ramp were deserted. The few
cabins that seemed habitable were closed and shuttered. A
store once operated here; you could mail a letter or make a
radio call, though most often the business transaction was
for a towel and a bath. There had been flowers in the window boxes then, cartons and canned goods on the shelves,
candy in jars by the cash register. Then a series of so-called
hundred-year storms hit, and later a bust in the fishing
economy. Now everything here was empty.

On the other side of the boardwalk was the bathhouse,
a tired wooden structure divided into a series of small
rooms. The tubs themselves, one to a room, were steel
cattle troughs, large ovals frosted with rust. From each
room came the sound of gushing water.

I took the first room with an open door and secured
it behind me as best I could with the wire hook. The

wooden floor was unswept, the window glass long since broken. Out the window, just feet away, scrub willow clung to a steep bank that was accented with rotting two-by-fours and discarded pipe.

The rusted steel tub was utterly unappealing, but the water was irresistible: clear, hot, always on, it splashed almost directly into the tub drain from a barely galvanized steel pipe. A hand-lettered sign on the wall was the only initiation. I did as directed: picked up the rag-wrapped rubber ball on a stick, which leaned against the corner, and stuffed it into the drain. The tub slowly began to fill. I undressed, piling my clothes carefully on top of my shoes to keep them off the dirty floor, balancing my towel on top. Before the tub was half-filled I stepped in and squatted in front of the pipe.

The temperature was perfect, absolutely, and the force of the stream enormously satisfying. I plunged my head underneath it, felt the water course through my hair, around my ears, over my neck and back and shoulders. The faint sulfur smell, far from being unpleasant, seemed pleasingly medicinal. It had been two days since I had washed more than my hands, and the sensation of water flowing over my body was a delicious massage.

What is it about water that comes hot out of the earth? Volcanism and tectonic plates can't explain the magic. In all places and all cultures, such water is considered healing, even sacred. To bathe in such water is a bounty.

The tub filled and filled. I ignored the rough rusted steel and lay back, eventually floating full length. My pubic hair fanned between my legs, my breasts flattened to my chest. For a moment I was weightless, the only sound the gush of water and my slow, deliberate breathing.

Taking a proper bath requires a suspension of rushing about and gotta-do-it. It requires patience, and—for me at least—a strange discipline to lie in the water and do nothing. Growing up with four siblings plus my parents and grandmother, I'd learned to be a survival bather: get in, get clean, get out, and don't use all the hot water. Amused and a little appalled, my roommates from college taught me one night how to take a proper bath, a languid half-hour soak with perfume and bubbles. But living aboard a sailboat for the last twenty years had almost obliterated their lesson, and I was back to a routine of three-minute showers. It's only when I step into a bath that I remember.

I sighed, releasing all of my breath, and sank below the surface.

Then, *No!* and I sat up, gasping. My mind raced, backward then forward then backward again, imagining someone—a man—on the other side of the door, waiting. I saw the flimsy latch, the rotted doorframe, the open window, the bare, dirty floor that was suddenly that other floor. I was caught, exposed and helpless, my nerves on the outside of my skin, as if I were flayed.

A whimper, the beginnings of a sob; I held my breath and listened, forcing myself to focus on what was around me rather than the clamor inside. All I could hear was rushing water and the blood pulsing in my ears. For a long moment I was submerged somewhere before or beyond time. I gathered everything, limbs, heart, all the fear. I opened my eyes and looked hard, clawing myself up to the present.

"I'm *here*," I said to the hot, unstoppable stream. "He's *there*." I made myself think of the rapist locked up, monitored, guarded, *watched*. I forced him into his cell. But there was something left that seemed to have its own life, slumbering in the margins of my spirit, waking when it would to grip my heart. What held me wasn't reality—I knew that—but it wasn't memory either, not if memory is recalling what happened years or even moments ago; what held me was remembering something that was happening *now*.

I inhaled and exhaled, deeply, deliberately, and slowly. *It's okay. You can do it.* I had to calm myself somehow, alone in this room. No way was I going back to *Eagle* like this. Still trembling, I bent forward until my head was under the streaming pipe. *Now, shampoo.* I slowly lathered my hair, my body. I pictured the boats rafted up in the blue harbor outside, the furled white sails; crews were waking one by one, some heading up the ramp, as Steve and I had. Where was he? Listening, I heard a door open, his friendly "good morning" as he passed others in the hall. I heard the easy voices of people arriving to bathe.

"Again," I said, rinsing and soaping. The bright morning returned.

A final submerge and rinse, and I was standing, watching the water swirl away, even as more kept flowing and flowing from somewhere in the mountains.

EVERYONE WAS UP and coffee was ready when I stepped across *Casa Mía* and aboard *Eagle*. Below, the cabin seemed more crowded than it ever had underway, full of broad shoulders and arms in motion, as if *Eagle* had some-how shrunk at the dock and could no longer contain five grown men. I stayed in the cockpit, which was already warmed by the sun and dried of dew.

Tim wanted no help whatsoever with breakfast. "You can do the dishes," he said from the hatch, handing me a paper plate blanketed to the rim with a single, brown, perfectly round pancake.

"Do you have any idea how weird it is?" I asked, ac-cepting with a slight bow and a big smile. "My not being allowed to cook?"

Frank passed me a mug of hot black coffee. Along with Larry, he and Tim had planned everything, and the three of them clearly enjoyed being cooks and servers. I liked that they didn't make a big deal about it but I wasn't entirely comfortable with my own role as designated eater. Normally I would be doing some or all of the cooking, especially on *Orca,* and while at times it was a chore now I was realizing that cooking was the one thing on this boat that I could do as well or better than the others, and I missed it. In so much else about this race I felt like an amateur; maybe what I really missed was being able to show off.

I was sipping my second cup of coffee when Larry was slowly hauled all the way up the forty-eight-foot mast in order to tune the rig; Mike's powerful muscles cranked the winch. From the top Larry hollered down his questions while Tim, Frank, and Steve yelled and gestured from below, periodically checking the results with binoculars.

The crew next to us on *Casa Mía* was keenly interested in the work going on at the top of *Eagle*'s mast. Tony, *Casa Mía*'s helmsman, had been on *Eagle* two years ago when she won the race and last year when she placed second. Both Tim and Frank spoke highly of Tony's sailing abilities, and the two boats had been competitive throughout the spring racing series. Yet the subject of our quitting was treated gently, as something unfortunate but not disastrous: too bad it happened; must have been a tough decision; glad you're going for the second leg. As it turned out, we wouldn't have been last in the first leg, as Frank had argued; three boats had pulled in after us. *Airloom,* the heavy cruiser, hadn't arrived yet.

No one threw this in our faces. Chris had said it all at the skippers' meeting: "We want to make this fun." Squinting in the sun, rafted cockpit to cockpit with the competing crew, their feet up as mine were, their hands curled around their coffee mugs, we were connected more by our shared pleasure than by a competitive spirit. The race seemed like an excuse to be here, as friends. Many of us knew one another anyway. Tony, the head of the extension college in Juneau, had been a student of mine in the beginning computing class I taught with Tim. Another of *Casa Mía*'s crew was a superior court judge in town, a friend of a friend. She had recently moved aboard her own boat and was, like me, new to this race. I'd heard about a third crew member, Bill, for years: a talented computer programmer, a dream to work with. Just now he had rolled out of his sleeping bag and had the look of a man who is trying, with all his might, to ignore the pounding headache of a hangover. Even at that, he smiled when we were introduced.

"Migael's lived aboard forever," he said to the others. "She's the saltiest person here." *Me?* I flashed back to myself cowering in the tub and had a sudden impulse to counter his opinion with the truth. *Yeah, sure,* I thought, *tell this nice guy the whole story, watch his face go slack and his eyes retreat in confusion and horror.* The word "rape" alone would darken the entire morning. It would be like throwing his compliment back at him.

Instead, I smiled and shook my head. "Oh, I'm not so tough as all that. It's you guys who are still living through Juneau winters! I only made it through four." A shared laugh, a gentle deflection of his generous words, and our conversation stayed on a smooth, effortless course. The others joined in and we talked about mutual friends, compared racing and cruising, joked about Juneau politics and working for the university. We talked and I found myself trying to look through Bill's eyes, bloodshot as they were, to catch a glimpse of the Migael he was seeing. The saltiest person there.

FRANK CALLED ME AWAY from *Casa Mia*. The rigging was tuned and it was time to practice.

From the moment we cast off, it was obvious that more than *Eagle*'s stays and shrouds had been adjusted. The first and biggest change was Steve. Tim and Frank had given him the job of tactician, putting him in charge of the sailing aspects of the race while they focused on overall strategy and navigation. Steve was clearly comfortable with the role.

His face was more expressive, his body larger and looser; it was as though, until now, he had been boxed up. Not that he became effusive or bossy. He simply stepped into the position with complete ease. It was expected. He'd been waiting.

And as if he sensed that we'd been waiting for him, Steve didn't waste a minute. The crew assignments he gave were absolute: one driver at the helm, one person on the foredeck, the rest of us on winches. Once the sail was set, everyone but the driver and tactician on the high side, legs over the rail. Our movements would be deliberate and smooth, all the time; too much jerking, too sudden a shift of weight from one side of the boat to the other and *Eagle* would lose speed. Even a fraction of a knot was too much.

"Come around in front of the mast," Steve yelled at Mike. "And keep your weight low." He put us through sail changes; we tacked against the wind and jibed with it.

"Migael! You're in charge of controlling the main when we jibe. Do it right and do it fast every time." I memorized the required motions as I did them: Release the preventer line (I reached for the line that held the boom, unclipping it from the toe rail). Center the main traveler (I adjusted the pulley that controlled the cluster of blocks that in turn controlled the angle of the main boom). Sheet in the main (I cranked the winch as *Eagle* changed direction and the sail began to luff, bringing the main toward the centerline). Ease it out after the jibe (I cupped the side of the winch with my hand and let the line slide through). Reattach the preventer. Crawl to the high side.

Tim and Frank still judged the new main to be not

quite right, but that didn't seem to matter so much now. We were correcting the balance between the six of us, sharpening our responses to each other, to *Eagle,* to the wind and seas. The conditions were perfect: a stiff breeze, a light chop on the water, brilliant sunshine. We couldn't count on any one of these to last. But the maneuvers Steve put us through, over and over, convinced us that we could count on ourselves.

It had always seemed to me that competitive sports were overrated, especially as character builders. I've heard too many stories to fall for the myth that the heroics of sporting transfer automatically to living. And, of course, in my high school and college years "real" sports were something guys did. I never played on a team then, barely considered sports a way to play at all. Until Juneau, when Joyce asked me to join a group of liveaboard women on a volleyball team. "Nothing serious," she explained, and from the start my attitude was more social than competitive. Our weekly games gave me a place to go when the evenings were long and dark; it was a mental as well as a physical release to run around inside a gym in shorts when the snow and slush outside were ankle deep. The beers we shared afterward mattered as much as the games, which we lost a little more often than we won. We were told that we could have been a fine team with practice and a coach; we accepted the compliment but never acted on the advice. We played strictly for fun.

Now I found myself on a real team and to my surprise it still felt like play. More like play in some ways than cruising, where I could never shake off the responsibility

for *Orca,* which I shared with Paul. Here on *Eagle* I had a
specific task, and perfecting that task made everything else
run more smoothly, whether I saw it or not. Seeing the
whole picture was Steve's responsibility. And I didn't take
his shouted commands personally; I wasn't flustered by
his yelling. Still thrifty with his opinions, he directed them
where they were needed and nowhere else. He was thrifty
with his praise as well, saving most of it for us as a team
rather than distributing it individually, in smaller pieces.
"We're doing it now," he'd shout. "We'll clean their clocks!"

Steve's competitive spirit was contagious, and the more
I practiced my small part the bigger I felt. For the first
time I wanted *Eagle*—us—to be ahead of the other boats.
I wanted to win. The outcome wasn't life and death or
profit and loss. The goal we were striving for was to simply
place respectably in the second leg of a sailing race so
remote that only a dozen or so boats signed up each year
and so insignificant that news of it rarely reached beyond
the sixty thousand residents of Southeast Alaska. This
race was important because we decided it would be, and
the fact that I could throw myself wholly into something
so pointless made me even more excited. I felt like a girl
on a playground, running from one side to the other for
the sheer joy of it; jump rope, jacks, and hopscotch were
reason enough to live.

I looked at the others on *Eagle,* ready to bet that right
now they were feeling a little like boys. Surely this was
what I had joined the race for, though I hadn't known it.
To feel like part of something bigger than myself, totally
and joyously. To move swiftly and synchronously. It was

work and attention, yet the smiles and even the frowns of concentration on all our faces were signs of pure pleasure.

All the confusion, indifference, and barely perceptible tension that followed yesterday's retirement from the race were gone, displaced by high spirits and a kind of resolve. The very contrast seemed to hone and bind us. And I had a feeling that this emerging teamwork, like the decision to quit the first leg, wouldn't be mentioned later. Each of us had been tuned, ratcheted tighter or looser. We handled lines, we cranked winches, we maintained our positions. We moved together.

FOR MUCH OF THE YEAR Warm Springs Bay is dull and gray, scuffed by rain. Even the forest loses its color. Gales from the Gulf of Alaska roar up and down Chatham Strait, seeking to invade the rocky entrance; usually the enraged water and wind are deflected by the high mountains. Clouds catch on the trees. The air, sodden and cool, seems to have weight. In winter, snow covers the beach, the dock, the boardwalk, then turns to slush, then to ice, then to slush again as temperatures hover above and below freezing. Occasionally a boat or a seaplane scuttles in— hunters, fishing crews, Forest Service rangers—attracted to the refuge of the dock and to the glorious hot water that never stops flowing.

But on this layover day, the dock was a festival. Sailboats rafted two deep at the dock. Sleeping bags aired over lifelines, flounces of green, blue, and red. By the time we returned from our practice sail, barbecues had already been set up, fishing poles rigged, and in everyone's hand there was a coffee cup or a can of beer, a soft drink or glass of wine.

Toward midafternoon, Tim was reading in the cockpit, Steve on the bow. Frank had already started cooking dinner; he shooed me away so cheerfully that it was clear he wanted to be alone.

"If you're up for a hike," Larry said as he laced his boots, "you're sure welcome to join us. We're heading up. There." He gestured with his chin to a peak some two thousand feet above us. Mike seconded Larry's invitation with a smile.

"Is there a trail?" I asked. Both of them reeked of insect repellant.

"We'll find one," Larry answered. Meaning they'd probably be bushwhacking most of the way. It would be an adventure, the view would be spectacular. A part of me wanted to go, another part of me hesitated. I could see them charging ahead, thigh and calf muscles working, me straining to keep up, inevitably slowing them down. Like the hikes Paul used to take me on when we were first dating. They turned out to be workouts.

"Thanks," I said, "but I'm feeling lazy today." Which was true, actually. Since our sailing practice a delicious languidness had spread through me, restorative as sleep, something I wanted to prolong rather than test. But I did need to stretch my legs. "I think I'll head up to the lake."

After they left, I changed into shorts, decisive all of a sudden, for the first time in days. The trail to the lake was well worn and other people would be coming and going often enough to keep bears from hanging around. I could go by myself, at my own pace.

Even in this long bout of warm weather, snow lingered on the high slopes of the mountains that crowded shoulder to shoulder over the bay. Walking, energized by the spring of the boardwalk, I felt almost naked in my shorts and tank top. Only two nights ago I'd been in thermal underwear and wool, gloved and hatted. There was something else too: a tingling over my body that I'd felt since the bath, as if all my senses were new and amplified. I seemed to have thrown off wariness like rain gear I no longer needed and without it I felt more, saw more. The rushing air at the falls was saturated with a sweetness I could smell through my skin. I looked downstream from the boardwalk; every few seconds the force of the roaring water sent the spray upwards into a patch of sunlight and for an instant the suspended droplets glowed like polished gems.

The trail up to the lake was a little muddy, interwoven with roots and studded with rocks that persisted in being underfoot. It was only a short walk, but it felt like a real hike. The shrubs, head high, were dense with tiny leaves and stiff branches. The spruce and cedar just beyond grew tall and close together. I could see the sky only by looking up.

At the lake I was greeted by a dozen other racers standing at the water's edge or sitting on logs, toes dangling. A few tried swimming but emerged gasping; the temperature at the surface was only slightly less frigid than the snowfields high above. A rowboat had been launched and was now in the middle of the lake, oars up, then down, dripping liquid silver.

I TOOK MY TIME returning to *Eagle,* walking slowly on the dock to get a good look at the competition. Talk about variety. Boats ranged from the twenty-five-foot production-line sloop *Northern Sails* to the forty-foot *Arrogant* with its home-built rigging, the two as mismatched as a motorcycle and a pickup. I wandered, smiling and chatting with owners and crew. Some had been racing every year since the Spirit of Adventure began. Others, like myself, were new. A few were racing with their kids and had even brought along their pets. I held out my open palm to a large, shaggy black dog and scratched behind his folded ears. "That's Digger," one of the crew said. "The high-side dog." Apparently Digger was so experienced a racer that he automatically went to the high side of the boat, as Steve insisted we do.

I'd loved being part of the boating community in Juneau. None of that big-boat/small-boat separation, which was so prevalent Down South—or sailboat/ powerboat, for that matter. Alaska has a way of destroying the sense of scale, and ultimately every boat was small. Other distinctions were blurred too; what someone did for a living wasn't nearly as important as their experience and their willingness to share it. Have you been in this or that cove and how was it going in? Can I make a tracing of your chart, copy figures from your tide tables? Can you spare an extra fuel filter? Got any scuba gear? Do you know anything about alternators? Diesel heaters?

Questions like these were asked far more often than "What do you do?"

Here in Warm Springs Bay, self-reliance and inter-dependence seemed perfectly balanced. It felt like a kind of Eden, though of course it was not. We were on a holiday, after all, and the long sunny day stretched before us, anchoring us in a present unconnected to tragedies or failures in the past, or to those ahead. For now, we could float on the bright surface, pretend that our stories were happy ones. Conversations were lighthearted by choice. No one I talked to probed for anything too personal or pointed, nor did I ask such questions of others, even on *Eagle*. I knew Tim was worried about his father, who was slowly going blind; he knew Paul and me well enough to sense that something was out of balance between us. Tim and I seemed to have agreed, without words, that this race would be a time out from our shore-bound lives. There in the sunlight of Warm Springs Bay it struck me that others had done the same.

People asked about Herm and Joyce, but under the bright blue sky it was hard to believe that Joyce was dead now, gone, with no more adventures ahead. So after the standard question about how Herm was doing ("Pretty good," was my reply), everyone set that hard subject aside.

Except for Dave, who I'd last seen hoisting the starting flag in Juneau Harbor and who I'd last heard over the radio crackle when we reported our position in Frederick Sound. He waved me aboard *Ariade* with a lift of his frosted glass. "Margarita?" he asked. I oohed and aahed over his roomy accommodations while the blender growled; as skipper of the committee boat for this race, he hadn't off-loaded the liveaboard clutter that makes a home out of a boat. What perfect therapy for his MS, I thought: a stable twin hull with lots of handholds; enough engine and enough sail combinations for solo cruising.

We stretched out in *Ariade*'s shaded cockpit. No need for Dave to bring up the subject of Joyce's death. The first leg of the race had only paused our brief conversation about her at the skippers' meeting, only strengthened our promise to really talk when we got here. We were silent for a moment, waiting, as if the story were an anchor that needed time to hook. We touched our glasses together. "To your health," we said, and meant it.

LOOKING BACK, it was a friendship that grew with each goodbye. The four of us—Paul and I, Herm and Joyce—had shared lots of good times during those years we lived in Juneau. But none of us, I think, realized how much we had in common until that spring when Joyce sold her boat and moved in with Herm on *Athena*. Things happened fast: They quit their jobs, they got married, they geared up to sail to Mexico. Paul and I were also leaving Alaska that summer for his new job in Seattle. Our impending trips down the Inside Passage brought the four of us closer together. We consumed whole evenings tracing possibilities on charts and discussing the minutiae of provisioning.

Seattle was the end of our voyage but only a stopping point for Herm and Joyce. They lingered one final evening in our marina, and over enchiladas we pretended we were

heading to Mexico with them. I remember the excitement
in Joyce's dark eyes when they cast off early the next morning, how she stood up from the bow where she was coiling
line to wave goodbye. Their last call was over the marine
radio, from just south of Port Townsend. "Good sailing to
you," I said over the airwaves. "*Orca* clear." The scratchy
transmission came back: "See you guys. *Athena* clear."

These were easy partings. Living on boats, we knew we
would share a mooring again, somewhere, someday. Over
the next year and a half, the cruising grapevine and one
letter told us about the snorkeling and fishing they were
enjoying in the Sea of Cortez. I didn't have the heart to
write back, to darken their clear skies and turquoise waters
with news of my attack. Of course, none of us knew what
was waiting for Joyce.

"THAT'S EXACTLY WHAT I want to do," broke in
Dave. "Next year, year after that at the latest, I'm heading south with *Ariade*." He spread his long arms to take in
his entire boat. "I'm *made* for Mexico." In his tropical shirt
he looked like he was already there. Dave's face, which
had just started to go slack with sadness, was animated
now, his eyes dancing as he described how he'd sail down,
harbor hopping all the way, how he'd kick back once he
got there. He said nothing about what he'd do if his MS
came back, nothing at all. It wasn't that he was foolhardy;
I knew him to be a careful boat handler who doesn't take
stupid risks. Maybe he was simply pretending that his MS
was gone. Maybe he had to in order to keep going. Or
maybe, listening to me talk about Joyce, he was reminded

of his own precarious health and inspired more than ever to try something new. I thought of asking but sensed that by asking I might disturb whatever balance he'd achieved, the way talking about a perfectly set sail somehow makes it luff and spill the wind.

That was the hard part, wasn't it? Finding that balance and trusting it. Light-headed all of a sudden—the tequila, already?—I swirled the crushed ice in my drink and continued on.

PAUL AND I HEARD about Joyce's cancer secondhand, through a mutual friend. A few weeks later Herm called. Amazingly, he first asked about me. He was so sorry for what had happened. He had just learned. How was I doing? By then over a year had passed since my attack and our lives had steadied. How could we help *them*? He was shipping *Athena* north the next day, flying to Seattle with Joyce. And once again we were caught up in their transition. Yes, there was moorage available in our marina. Yes, we'd arrange it for them.

Soon after they arrived Joyce went into the hospital for exploratory surgery. We all knew the odds. Almost no one survives ovarian cancer. But they're called odds for a reason—some do make it—and we chose to believe that Joyce could be one of them. Our hopes seemed justified when she regained her strength and even her appetite after returning to *Athena*. And the biopsy news three months later was the best possible: no cancer anywhere.

Our friendship ripened that following summer, Paul and me on *Orca,* Herm and Joyce a hundred feet away on

Athena. Joyce found work as a lab technician in a nearby hospital. She and Herm repaired their inflatable, took apart their diesel stove, tiled the wall behind it. During our evening walks together the two of them talked about selling *Athena,* buying a house. Joyce wanted a garden. She wanted to see things grow.

But by early fall Joyce was slowing down. "I'm so tired of being tired," she told me. "Herm wants me to be more energetic, but I'm just not." For the first time she spoke about her own grim chances. "I know what those blood tests mean," she said. "And lately mine have been looking scary." Periodically she'd remark on how few women survive this type of cancer, how short their lives are after it's diagnosed.

"That doesn't mean it'll happen to you, Joyce," Herm would be quick to say; like Paul, he seemed always fixed on the positive, a compass pointing true north. But a sadness was beginning to set in behind his eyes and in the corners of his mouth. Death was in the shadows of our conversations.

"I hate it when people insinuate that I have cancer because I didn't eat right," Joyce said one evening as we were sharing a chicken dinner. It was her chicken, prepared with flavor and flair, Joyce being one of the best cooks I've known.

"Yeah," I said. Why did people *say* things like that? When something devastating strikes out of nowhere, stops you midpassage, you look back endlessly for clues to explain why it happened. You blame yourself enough. Besides, criticizing Joyce for living an unhealthy life was absurd. If the cause was as simple as stress or the wrong foods, I was the one who should have cancer. "I've been meaning to talk to you about that, Joyce. How come you never ate enough Brussels sprouts?" I turned to Paul and Herm. "Where are those sprouts?" They feigned a frantic search under the galley table. "*We* have Brussels sprouts every day."

Joyce giggled, delighted by our joking. I loved her laugh, bouncy, like her dark brown curls.

"To hell with them," Paul said. He sopped up the chicken juice on his plate with a slice of sourdough bread. "You don't need to hear that. They're just trying to convince themselves that cancer will never happen to them, as if anybody could predict it. To hell with them." His voice was angry and a look passed over his face that jarred me back ten years, to a late evening in a hospital when Paul himself was scheduled for surgery the next morning. They would open his chest, spread his ribs, remove what was suspected to be cancer but turned out to be a harmless cyst. That look—haunted, bravely hopeful—had lingered in his eyes for a long, long time.

"SO IT WAS ONLY a remission."

I recoiled at the sound of Dave's voice, startled, and realized at once that I'd lost myself in the memory of Paul's cancer scare. How could I have forgotten so much about that anxious time? There it was, nested inside my memory of Joyce's dinner, waiting for me to discover it in the telling.

Dave reached for the blender and refilled our empty glasses.

"Yeah," I sighed. "The cancer came back." I hated saying those words. Telling this whole story was hard; it was stirring things up. And the ending—I didn't want to tell that either. And what about Dave? Jesus. For him, listening was probably harder. He seemed to have triumphed over multiple sclerosis, but had he really? Did anyone? To live with the knowledge that you carried something inside you that might end your life—it was like carrying an explosive you couldn't defuse, that something malignant or indifferent had the power to detonate.

"But you know," I continued, eager to reassure him, eager to reassure *me*, "she was still Joyce." Yes, she had gone back into the hospital that November, and yes, her belly had been full of cancer. But somehow she exuded the same calm directness she'd always had, whether sailing or scrubbing a hull; one was a pleasure, the other a chore, but you couldn't have one without the other. I never heard her complain, though she did miss living aboard when she and Herm moved ashore, just as she missed her own spicy cooking when her medication became complex and her diet bland. She tried to get outside every day and as always she noted the small things—the mosaic of leaves on the sidewalk or the way a squirrel scrabbled up a tree—as if the details of ordinary living would keep her alive.

It was a shimmering, holding-still time, like water at slack current, like air just before the wind changes direction. It couldn't last.

Joyce had always been the better sailor, Herm said. She knew before he did when to reduce sail. She started talking about her family, about going to Arizona where they lived. She was cold in Seattle now—this woman who had thrived in Alaska—and wistfully described the dry heat of the desert.

Within a month Joyce was back in the hospital to have more fluid drained from her bulging abdomen. The cancer was everywhere. It wouldn't be long. Herm's voice over the phone was stiff and tight. As soon as Joyce had enough strength they were flying to Arizona.

Paul and I drove to the hospital that afternoon. We had no idea what we would say when we got there, no idea what she would look like. All we knew was that we had to see her, touch her. We had to get close.

What struck me wasn't Joyce's appearance but the room's. It was utterly, completely empty. No flowers, no cards. Joyce lay on white sheets under a white blanket. Her dark hair framed her pale, almost translucent skin. A clear tube snaked into her right nostril. Beside her on the bedside tray were just two items: a white Bible with gilded pages and a large bottle of expensive perfume.

Paul and I sat on either side of her. We talked of trivial things: Where'd she get the Bible? How was her belly feeling? When was she leaving for Arizona? I unscrewed the cap of her perfume bottle and breathed the delicate fragrance.

Then something crested, curled, broke the surface, and at the same time Paul and I reached for Joyce, almost crawled into the hospital bed with her. We rocked and cried, the three of us. What words were left?

"I'm going to miss you guys." Joyce's embrace was weak, but her voice and her clean tears seemed strong. "Thanks for saying goodbye."

So in the end all we could send her off with was our sorrow. We missed, by minutes, her departure the next day to Arizona. By the time we arrived at the hospital she had already checked out, transfused with two pints of blood in order to make the flight south. Inland, away from the sea.

During the next month I called her periodically. I'd ask her to describe the scene outside her window, the cactus and the sun and the dry air. She was surrounded by family there and in her voice I could hear the love she was receiving.

It was late one evening in early March when the call came. We first saw the message as a blinking red light on our answering machine. I pushed the play button. In the darkness a flat voice came through the tiny speaker like the voice on our marine radio long ago. "This is Herm. Joyce passed away this evening. I wanted you guys to know." A pause, almost like a sob. "*Athena* clear."

"THERE WAS NO VEAL in Juneau," Frank announced as he piled beef stroganoff, fragrant with wine and onions, over a mountain of flat noodles. His apology for not making veal Marsala was unnecessary, to say the least. Frank had been cooking since three in the afternoon, red apron spread across his belly, Eagle embroidered on the bib—another gift, this one from Tim's father, who apparently knew what Frank's real passion was. It was obvious from the French bread pulled from the gimbaled oven, the fresh green beans, the apple pie waiting on the chart table, that Frank had been doing exactly what he wanted. The limits of the tiny galley made his accomplishment all the more fun and satisfying.

Outside, in the still-bright evening, the smells of meals from the other boats mingled with ours. All the crews were below now, as we were, crowded around narrow tables, savoring what would be bragged about over the bonfire later, as though the quality of the food were a factor in determining the winner of the race.

We ate for a while in silence. Our faces were flushed with sunburn, and around our eyes was a raccoon mask of white from the shade of sunglasses. My hair hung limp and straight, creased at ear level by the Eagle cap I'd worn all day. Tim, Larry, and Steve, normally clean shaven, were now stubbled. Frank's beard grew thickest, like his almost-black curls; he scratched his chin. Mike's was the least noticeable. We sat shoulder to shoulder, three to a side; *Eagle* enclosed us like an egg.

"Did any of you guys get aboard *Silver Girl* today?" I asked between mouthfuls of stroganoff so delicious my eyes watered. The guys shook their heads. "It's completely empty inside," I said. "I mean *empty*. Beautiful woodwork, floors you could eat off, but nothing in it. No sign of the crew." Unlike *Eagle*. Around us was a tumble of sleeping bags, duffels, sweaters, and jackets. The galley was a riot of dirty pans. "Keith"—Frank grunted when I named *Silver Girl*'s skipper—"acted like a salesman, showing off the electronics and the sound system. I asked him where the crew slept and get this—no one's allowed below during the race. Not even to *sleep.*"

Everyone but Steve looked up and stopped eating. "You mean they sleep *outside?*" asked Tim.

"Outside." I leaned forward over my plate. "On the *high* side."

Steve was still eating. "I'm not at all surprised," he said. "It's the way we operate. Not for the really long races," he assured us. "But a race like this, with good weather, light airs, just one night out on each leg—yeah, everyone's outside pretty much all the time, on watch or off. It can make a difference."

I silently calculated the weight of six to eight racers, usually men weighing 180 pounds each. Below, even half of those men, plus the weight of their gear and food, could settle a boat down in the water. This might be okay running with the wind when the hull was level, but on a tack too much weight below in the wrong place would only exaggerate the boat's heel to port or starboard, increasing the wetted surface of her hull, increasing the friction of water that would slow her down. A fraction of a knot over a twenty-four-hour period—Steve had a good point.

"I think I speak for all of us," said Larry, his eyes twinkling at Frank, "when I say that we're real glad you and Tim don't race that way." He reached for the French bread, tore off a chunk. "You can bet the guys on *Silver Girl* aren't eating like we are. I've been looking forward to this meal for a week."

Frank brightened and patted his round belly. "Can

you imagine me on *Silver Girl*? Keith probably has a weigh-
in test."

"The guy's out of place." Steve put down his fork and
his voice was hard. "This just isn't that kind of race. He
makes me want to bring *Bandito* up here next year and suck
the doors off *Silver Girl*."

We laughed at the thought of Steve's forty-four-foot
C & C, with its tested, professional crew, leaving *Silver
Girl* behind in its wake. But why would Steve bother? The
revenge would be so silly. Steve had just nailed it—this
truly *wasn't* that kind of race. He could have added, though
he didn't, that the low rating Keith insisted on at the skippers' meeting practically assured his win. In this setting,
with these boats and especially these boaters, *Silver Girl* was
proving nothing that we didn't already know. She might as
well be racing by herself.

ALL THE SUN, all the cross-boat conversations, to say
nothing of Frank's dinner, took their toll. We all showed
up at the bonfire, but I didn't stay long. One by one the
others followed me back to *Eagle*. Frank, Tim, and Steve
talked strategy in the cockpit for a while. Larry thumped
around on the foredeck, arranging sail bags into a mattress. Finally we were all in our berths: Frank and Mike in
the triangular forepeak, me on the port side of the main
cabin, Steve to starboard. Aft, in the quarter berth tucked
beneath the cockpit bench, was Tim. I closed my eyes in
the dim light and slept.

It was a little lighter, but still early by my watch—three
o'clock—when I awoke. What was that noise? As soon as I

formed the question I knew: Every man below was sleeping soundly, and every one of them was snoring. Each, I
gradually noted, had a different tone and tempo. Steve,
whose voice was lowest, snored a baritone. Tim's ended
with a whistle, Frank's with a snort. Mike, the youngest,
was the tenor. I lay in the middle of this stereophonic
performance, fascinated.

I've never slept with a snorer, at least not one I couldn't
stop with a poke. But here I was, sleeping with four of
them, in what was essentially one room. I was wide awake
now, alert to each rasping tune, mildly annoyed. I couldn't
tiptoe from berth to berth, shaking each man in turn until
he cleared his throat, turned, and was breathing silently
in sleep. So I listened, imagined Larry topside on his mattress of sails and all the men on all the boats sending a
chorus of snores outward into the hushed, amazed wild.

The absurdity hit me and I almost laughed out loud.
Here I'd been worried about being the only woman aboard,
wondering how I'd fit in with a boat full of guys, and the
only real problem I'd encountered was this: The men
snored. In every other way they were crew, team members,
friends. Cooks and captains. Quitters and starters. Fellow
voyagers around Admiralty Island.

A knot inside me loosened, and as if their snores were
a giant's lullaby I drifted back toward sleep.

THE BED PAUL AND I SHARE is shaped like a piano.
A little narrower, about as long, positioned fore and aft in
the back cabin. One side follows the curve of Orca's hull
to the transom, where it squares off to meet the straighter

side of the bed. The headboard is part of the bulkhead—
one of many interior walls that strengthen *Orca*'s hull.

Paul and I sleep with our heads and shoulders at
the wide end, toes pointing aft. Lying there, my body at
Orca's waterline, I can touch the ceiling overhead without
straightening my arms, feel the soft give of the water even
on a calm night, like the sag and sway of a hammock, as if
cradled by something alive.

Usually we moor *Orca* bow-southward to meet prevail-
ing southerlies—the direction most storms come from
on the north Pacific coast. Her head, like ours, faces south,
taking the wind and the fetch of wave on her bow as she
was designed to do. When the wind blows from the north,
the water breaks against her broad, flat transom with
gurgles, clicks, and pops, almost as though she were being
tickled, or it slams hard, not six feet from our heads.

Gales from any direction are impossible to sleep through.
The wind moans low and deep, high up in the rigging. The
stays and shrouds whine, and the mast thrums. The rain is a
shower of pebbles on the deck above us. We snuggle under
the blankets and wait it out.

For over fifteen years we've slept like this and it has
never felt crowded. Quite the opposite; when we sleep on
land, even an ordinary double bed seems huge. We do get
a kick out of all the room—it makes us want to jump up
and down on the mattress—but by morning we end up on
one side, having moved toward each other in the night.
I've come to need this closeness in order to sleep deeply
and well, even if it's only an intertwining of our feet, the
top of my forehead against Paul's back, the rearranging of

limbs when one of us rolls over. When Paul gets up in the morning before me, I roll to his side of the bed, embracing his pillow, inhaling his scent.

In the numbness immediately after I was raped, I lay stiff in bed, covered neck to toe in my nightgown, enclosed by Paul's arms and *Orca*'s ribs. Far, far sooner than either of us expected, I relaxed in this double embrace. My need for Paul's touch became a craving that astonished us both. It was as though the violence had left tracks on my body that could only be healed by gentleness, like the scar of a deep wound that must be massaged over months and years before it gives up its redness. My desire was tactile as much as sexual; my very skin was hungry. Only in the last year has the hunger quieted.

Still, the memories arise, more from my body than from my mind, as they did this morning in the bath. Memories that stop time and rewind it until I am there, alone, trapped between dying and living, as if my neck had never been released.

I sighed for the reassurance of Paul's body and turned in the narrow berth. Nothing for it now. I was on *Eagle*, in Warm Springs Bay, on the east side of Baranof Island. A roadless range of mountains stood between me and the nearest airport in Sitka. The nearest telephone I knew of was fifty miles south, at Port Alexander. *Well, what did you expect?*

I didn't have to wonder what Paul would be thinking about in the unlikely event that he was awake at this hour. He would briefly imagine me sleeping aboard *Eagle*. Had we made it to the layover yet? Were we still underway? Then,

as always, he would turn to something sure and solid.
His mind would fill happily with construction details.
Somewhere in a floor plan or a wiring diagram he would
fall asleep.

How I envied that ability of his! Something would
fall apart and Paul's first instinct was to fix it. Well,
maybe not *it,* the specific thing that had been damaged,
but some *thing* would be repaired, or built, or changed. I
remembered how he'd changed jobs soon after his surgery,
how knowing he *didn't* have cancer made him want to try
something new—a small architectural firm instead of a
large one—and when that didn't work how eager he was to
cruise to Alaska. It was no wonder he'd leapt at the chance
to rebuild the house. At last, a way to provide for his
mother now that his father was dead. A way to connect to
his father as well. During the rebuilding, we were always
discovering carpenter pencils carved with his dad's name,
studs he'd obviously scavenged from an even older structure, plumbing that was as baffling and ingenious as his
mind. I smiled, thinking how much of his dad was in Paul.
The house was Paul's way of shaping something of himself
too, a way for him to *be.* I'd loved him for this when we
first started dating, his eagerness to build tangible, useful
objects—a kayak, a shelf, a set of speaker boxes—and then
to make them better.

No, the house wasn't pulling Paul and me apart, though
I'd been looking at it that way, seeing it, as I saw everything,
through the shattered lens of my attack. In the early light
aboard *Eagle* I felt as if my vision was just beginning to clear.
There was something else too, something important in the

distance, but it skittered away when I tried to focus on it. Like a shooting star, small and bright against the dark, best seen on the periphery or in motion.

OVER THE YEARS, WE'VE watched friends move out of marriages, some amicably, most painfully. Forces had worked on them, separately and together. We've always known that similar forces could work on us.

Not that anyone was noticing. From the outside Paul and I looked like an ideal couple. Hadn't we built our boat together? Survived a crisis that destroys most marriages? But destruction doesn't have to be dramatic. What I was feeling was something as silent as carpenter ants invading a foundation—just a few at a time, then a nest, then a gnawing at the timbers from within. Until one day you're doing something so ordinary, opening a window or closing a door, and you notice the latch is loose, looser than all the other times, in fact it pulls right out, screws and all, and the wood smells wet and rotten. That's what I was afraid of for us, the quiet eating away.

ORCA HAS TAUGHT US many things, and one of them is this: If you want something to last, don't ignore the early signs of wear.

Water and air and everything alive in them work inexorably to tear down a boat. Ten years after we laid *Orca*'s keel and felt we were pretty much finished, the rot began. Alaska accelerated the process: a freeze and a seam would be pushed open, ever so slightly; a thaw and water seeped in more deeply. A freeze again. The wood never dried. Spores of rot germinated and spread. What had been sound, sweet-smelling, dry, and golden turned mushy and black.

Of course there were signs that the protective shell around us was giving way but we were too busy to pay much attention to the baffling drip here and there or the dampness in a locker. When the weather in Juneau was good we wanted to go sailing or fishing. An annual haul-out, a squirt of caulking, cosmetic varnishing and painting—that was all the maintenance we took time for.

It was only when we returned to the relatively dry climate of Seattle that we faced the fact that *Orca* was rotting. If she was to last, we would have to do some serious work: tear off the cabin, trace out every vein of rot, and replace with new.

Tearing down was hardest. This was plywood we had soaked with preservatives, bedded and screwed and sealed once and for all, we thought. It made a sickening, splitting sound as we pried it from *Orca*'s steel frames. We had to destroy so much healthy wood in order to remove what was rotten.

The work was disheartening, but when it was done— when the cabin had been rebuilt, every seam sealed and bedded, every screw tapped, driven, and plugged, the sides repainted, the teak revarnished—when it was done, Paul and I felt relieved and satisfied. *Orca* was good as new.

Then winter, and the rains came, and violence like a sudden storm, and we were capsized.

I HADN'T KNOWN WHAT to say that afternoon last autumn. I thought Paul was napping, but as I was reading in the pilothouse I heard something soft, a kind of gasp, and when I went down into the main cabin I saw that he was crying. I lay down next to him, held him, tried to cover him with my body. "Did you have a bad dream?" I asked.

"You're going to change, I just know it." He cried. His arms tightened around me. "You're going to change and then you'll leave."

Stunned, I kissed him, over and over, his forehead, his mouth, his beard. "No. Never."

Even as he kissed me back, he kept shaking his head. "You are. You are."

LIFTED

A FRESH WIND BLEW in from the entrance of Warm Springs Bay, making the water dance. Everyone on every boat was moving at a stepped-up pace this morning, preparing for the second leg of the race. The dock was covered with sails that, one by one, were inspected, folded, and packed. Engines spit exhaust and water, charging batteries. The only person standing around was the editor of *Sailing World,* and he was busy snapping photographs, changing lenses, writing down names. The auto advance on his camera whirred.

I was below on *Eagle,* stowing gear with Mike. Six adults—and none of us were slobs by a long shot—can generate a surprising amount of clutter on a thirty-four-foot sailboat. In only one day we had spread our junk over every horizontal surface. Coffee mugs had sprouted from the settees. Tubes of sunblock had slithered onto the floor. Jackets had cloned themselves on the berths. Together Mike and I herded up as much as we could, then he went forward to clean the head. I focused on the galley.

I enjoy putting the chaos of a galley in order. Wiping

down counters and clearing the sink always gives my thoughts more room. As I slid the washed dishes into their rack, dropped the salt and pepper shakers into their storage holes, sorted the utensils into their narrow bins in the tiny drawer, I felt like I was fitting pieces into a three-dimensional puzzle. I was absorbed, my limbs moving as sure and quick as thought.

Before long I was topside, helping Mike and Larry with the lines. Every sheet had to be uncoiled and laid along the deck in order to relax twists that might become hazardous snarls under tension, to work out the kinks Tim called hockles, but which Paul—I grinned, remembering—always referred to as assholes; they had a maddening tendency to jam a block. We recoiled each line, letting its natural lay guide our hands.

While Frank was fussing over the engine, Tim and Steve adjusted the standing rigging, then double-checked everything. The three of them briefly conferred below, gesturing and tracing circles over the chart. Then all of us were on deck, casting off.

Frank cut the engine as soon as we cleared the entrance and at the same moment Larry and Mike raised the main, then the number 2 genoa. Tim and I winched in the sheets. Steve was at the wheel. We moved to our tasks smoothly and swiftly, separate gears engaging one another. *Eagle* lifted her bow and ran.

This time we headed for the start smoothly and aggressively. Beating into the stiff southerly breeze, we approached the committee boat from the north. Tim explained our strategy: we would pass *Ariade* seconds before noon, as close as we could, then smartly jibe for a downwind start the instant the flag was dropped.

Every boat in the race converged at full speed toward *Ariade*. My instinct was to give way; I could hear my neighbor Ole's voice from years ago, thick with its Norwegian accent: *Right of way is something you give, not something you take.* But what held for tugs and fishing vessels apparently didn't hold for racing sailboats. Steve's hands never wavered on the wheel.

"Sheet in, Migael," he said, and I cranked in the main, increasing our speed upwind. Beside us was *Casa Mía,* nose to nose not ten feet away. Tony grinned a challenge from her helm and both Tim and Frank jokingly shook their fists. Steve kept his attention forward, as if *Casa Mía* didn't matter. Perhaps she didn't; we had the right of way.

The distance between us closed. Neither boat gave way. The starting flag dropped, and we both jibed, rounding *Ariade. Casa Mía* held her course; we held ours. The jibe, perfectly executed as it was, had pointed *Eagle's* head directly at the committee boat. *Ariade* was in our path, dead ahead.

I shot a questioning glance at Steve, who surely saw what was about to happen. What good was our position now? Perhaps he had a trick up his sleeve; perhaps at that moment he was about to order us to fall off. In any case, *Ariade* took action first: Dave scrambled into the pilothouse and powered backward to avoid a collision.

"Seven-twenty *Eagle!*" chimed the crews on the other boats. *What?* There was no time to ask for an explanation. Without a grumble Steve immediately ordered two 360 degree turns as the fleet sailed past.

Right then, yesterday's practice paid off as we sailed
Eagle through two clean full circles that made me feel like
an expert on the main boom. Before the second was complete, Larry and Tim raised the spinnaker. It ballooned
instantly with red, white, and blue stripes that soared
beyond the mast.

"Barging," Larry explained as he sat next to me amidships on the high, port side. *"Ariade* shouldn't have had to
move. We take our penalty now and it's over with."

I nodded at his explanation. This 720 rule—I liked it.
Instead of waiting until after the race for a protest to be
made against us and our placement adjusted accordingly,
we'd been fined on the spot. The dispute had been settled
then and there, and we could get on with the race. The fine
was a serious one; it had taken precious time to turn *Eagle*
twice around. But though we'd lost momentum we hadn't
lost morale. Already we were catching up with the fleet.

Spinnakers—light as air, striped with color—blossomed
from every bow. Legs dangled over every hull. The wind, at
our backs now, was warm and steady from the south. Our
wake gurgled behind us—an immensely satisfying sound.

A whoosh of water and air, and everyone turned their
heads. Approaching from the east were two plumes, one
high, one low: a humpback whale and her calf. Every
few seconds the broad, glossy black hump of the mother
emerged, and at the same instant the smaller hump of her
baby. They swam rhythmically toward us, then turned
to parallel our course, not fifty yards away. Their breaths
were perfectly timed.

I had forgotten this feeling: a wild happiness, a flooding

peace. To be this close to a humpback whale, to be approached, as this mother and calf were approaching now. The plumes we had seen at a distance on Frederick Sound had been lovely, but this! It was as if we were being chosen for something, made larger. Not that we could see much. Except when they're breaching—and then their long bodies stream with foam that covers them like a caul—humpbacks reveal little of themselves. A fin, a dorsal and blowhole, perfect flukes. Your imagination fills in the rest, and your imagination is never big enough.

I've always considered the whales my reward for staying those years in Southeast Alaska. We would have been long gone back to Seattle that mid-September weekend, before the October gales settled in or the termination dust—that early snowfall—moved down the mountains. Instead, having decided to winter over in Juneau, we were anchored off Admiralty Island. All that still afternoon, in the crystal light, we watched, dumbfounded, as a half dozen humpback whales surfaced and bellowed around us. They raised their knobby, winglike fins, holding them skyward for minutes at a time, as if waving. They stood on their heads and lobbed their enormous tails back and forth in thunderous slaps that echoed off the mountains. They groaned and grunted and snorted. How could anything be so huge and so supple at the same time? Of course the spectacular show had nothing to do with us; there was no intermission when we raised anchor and headed back to Juneau. Perhaps they continued all night. Were they playing? Fighting? Feeding? Singing? Impossible to know for sure.

For all the study that's been done on these whales, for all the hydrophones lowered to record their complex sounds, for all the underwater photography and patient research, very little is known. Every time I encounter them in the wild, I seem to learn less. Whales generally avoid boats, I read, and then one summer it seemed as if they were seeking us out, sounding beneath our hull, surfacing so close we inhaled their fishy breath. Or we'd find ourselves waiting off the fuel dock for a humpback to leave; didn't it know that it wasn't supposed to like it there? Gentle giants? A friend of ours was nearly capsized by a humpback as he rowed up Gastineau Channel, and that same year several fishing boats were hit. Was it the same whale or many? Angry, playful, or simply inattentive? Some say a deep-draft boat like ours, under sail, attracts whales, who see the hull underwater as something akin to them. At twenty-five tons, *Orca* weighs in at about average for a humpback, but how stiff she must seem, and how ignorant of whale etiquette. Whatever that is.

It was only after cruising Alaska that I came to appreciate *Moby Dick,* that prodigious volume every English major was required to read in college. I understood, finally, why Melville went on and on about this anatomical part and that—every muscle, sinew, and bone. He made mistakes (he was convinced whales were fish, for example, not mammals) but much of what we know, he knew: the sinuous trails of their migrations, their courtships, their fierce defense of young and wounded, their long lives. In page after page of prose he exhausted the English

language, trying to describe what is still so unknowable.
In the end, not even all his words could encompass one
single whale.

So the most fitting response to seeing a whale was the
response we had on *Eagle:* a gasp, then silence.

"OF COURSE, THE WHALE is God." I could hear the
professor's sonorous declaration in my American lit class.
No doubt I wrote his words dutifully in my notes. Now
I would cross them out. For me the whale is of *this* world,
not some other. Huge, powerful, and strangely vulnerable,
it breathes air, yet stranded and aground and surrounded
by air it suffocates. Close up the whale is thrilling, wildly
so, and the thrill is part exhilaration and part fear. The
whale can display itself gloriously or take me right under,
where I cannot breathe. Part of me needs to stay at a distance that's safe. Part of me longs to get closer.

IT WASN'T LONG AFTER the whale and her calf
changed course and left us that Tim noticed a sailboat
far behind, near the entrance to Warm Springs Bay. He
reached below for the binoculars, raised them to his eyes.
"Airloom," he said. He put the binoculars down, and then
looked through them again as if he didn't quite believe
what he'd seen.

Frank turned on the radio and through the crackle we
heard *Airloom's* skipper reporting in to the committee boat.
She had gamely sailed the entire first leg and was just now
entering Warm Springs Bay. She would join us later, after
baths and a meal.

"Did you hear that?" Frank shouted from the hatch, and he repeated the news. We listened, smiling at each other. The retelling made it even better. The heavy-displacement ketch we'd last seen at the start of the first leg, the one all the rest of us could so easily outsail in light air, hadn't given up. *Airloom* was still in the race.

TOWARD LATE AFTERNOON, the southerly brought in a high overcast and the low-pressure system spawned that morning in the Gulf of Alaska steadily worsened. The wind rose to a low howl. The seas changed from dancing ripples to lively whitecaps to streaked waves that broke in hissing crests. Behind us the water was dark and gray: twenty-five knots of wind and rising.

Eagle lifted, almost surfing down the front of the break-ing crest. I looked at Tim and Frank; their faces were tight. Downwind at this speed under spinnaker is a difficult point of sail. A boat can easily go too fast, faster than the wave, then broach, her bow digging in and pivoting her to windward. Or be swamped by a following sea. Or—most extreme—pitchpole, flipping end for end.

The spinnaker jerked and dipped like a kite, no longer beautiful and cloudlike but a threatening, misshapen thing. Standing now with legs apart, Tim worked the wheel back and forth, trying to keep *Eagle*'s fin keel perpendicular to the seas and her bow up. If she was caught sideways with a full spinnaker, a knockdown was likely.

"Know what to do if she starts to broach?" Steve asked Frank. I was clinging to the cockpit coaming, trying not to look at the seas piling behind us. At the sound of Steve's voice—utterly controlled—I realized I had forgotten to exhale.

"Release the sheet," Frank replied.

"Less action," Steve said to Tim. "Don't work the rudder so much. Migael, release the main a bit more. Larry, Mike—that pole needs to be raised at the mast." They crawled up to the pitching bow.

Jesus, I thought, moving to his orders. *He's making us go faster.* I could feel my stomach knot, and it wasn't seasickness causing it this time.

The wind and seas kept rising. It would be dusky—almost dark with these clouds—in a couple hours. We raced on.

Suddenly *Eagle* pivoted. For an instant she was weightless, as though about to dive, or fly, or fall. Her stern reared up—too far—then slid sideways. Everything shuddered as the boom swept the deck, starboard to port, as far as the preventer would allow, then back again. The noise, though brief, was horrendous: the dull snap of the mainsheet tightening, the rattle of blocks, the mainsail filling with a thud as if it had been struck. All these sounds at once, and the howling wind and the hiss of breaking crests.

"Don't oversteer!" Steve yelled at Tim, who was gripping the wheel. "I get *real* nervous when that happens!" *Eagle* had recovered; Tim had put her back on course, Frank had released the sheet, though I hadn't seen any of this. In the moment of that accidental jibe I'd braced myself—or had I been thrown?—against the cockpit seat; I'd watched the preventer, willing it to hold fast.

Tim bit his lip and continued steering, his eyes darting

up, ahead, side to side. "I'd feel better if you took the wheel," he said to Steve after what seemed like a long pause. Without a word the two traded positions. The rest of us stayed where we were, crouched in the cockpit or on the cabin, gripping a cleat or a shroud. *Handhold religion:* The old mariner's term perfectly described our fervent postures, and as soon as those two words came to mind the muscles around my eyes and mouth inexplicably relaxed.

More than *Eagle*'s rigging and hull had been strained in those chaotic seconds. I could feel my body and brain flushed with adrenaline, all my senses enlarged. Had I looked at Larry and Mike, I felt sure I would have seen the same dilated eyes, the same complete attention, the same readiness to act.

"Look," said Steve. His voice was calm again. "We're working too hard here. Why don't we head west a bit into quieter water, catch our breath?" At Tim's nod he eased the wheel to port. At the same time Frank and Tim adjusted the spinnaker sheets while Mike winched in the main—"not too much," Steve warned—and I readjusted the preventer.

It took less work and attention to reach across Chatham Strait than to sail downwind—less danger of jibing accidentally again. But the spinnaker was still skittish. *Eagle* was barely in control.

"I'm getting too old for this shit," Tim said finally. "It's getting darker and the weather's getting worse." Frank nodded agreement. "As soon as it's safe we're dropping the spinnaker."

Thank God. When Tim had passed the wheel to Steve,

it had been only an assignment; he hadn't given up command. Now he and Frank had seen what it was their job as skippers to see, that we'd reached the limit of our skill with the spinnaker. I'd known that I was over my head when the first stiff gust dipped that huge sail. It was a relief to know the others weren't so far behind.

We still had to douse *Eagle*'s spinnaker, a tricky maneuver in conditions like these. Steve talked us through it first, then stayed at the wheel while Frank and Tim joined Larry on the foredeck. Mike and I worked the lines in the cockpit, keeping the main in position so it blanketed the spinnaker, and the smoothness of my own movements surprised me. The fear that was making my heart pound didn't immobilize me at all, not like that time way up Lynn Canal, when it was blowing sixty knots and Paul and I had to get the storm jib down and we did it all right, but afterward my hands were numb and shaking and I was so cold. This was more like a stillness inside that slowed time so that everything I needed to see I saw completely and everything I needed to do I did with care. I felt a kindred focus and alertness in the others as well, as if we were all hearing the same backbeat, moving to the same rhythm.

YEARS AGO, TEACHING JOURNALISM in high school, I'd brought in a friend to be interviewed. He climbed radio and TV towers for a living, checking the lights and electrical connections for the various stations broadcasting around Seattle. He climbed using the steel of the tower for handholds and footholds—there was rarely a ladder—and a short tether on his safety belt that he clipped and unclipped a thousand times. The towers rose hundreds of feet in the air.

My students were fascinated. "Look at his arms!" one whispered, and I had to admit he looked pretty invincible.

"Are you ever afraid of falling?" another asked toward the end of the interview.

"Of course!" he answered, incredulous. "All the way up I'm afraid of falling, and all the way down. When I'm on those towers, fear is my *friend.*"

THE SPINNAKER DOWN, we raised the number 2 genoa, and *Eagle* relaxed into a swift, controlled reach across Chatham Strait. The wind and seas we had been struggling against became our allies, pushing us north, around Admiralty.

Chatham Strait is consistently narrow—some ten miles across all the way from Frederick Sound north to Icy Strait, mountains on both sides. With the light slanting through the western clouds, Baranof Island, layered with gray and violet peaks, seemed a jumble of separate islands, enticing us with silvered fjords. To the east, Admiralty Island presented an equally steep but less convoluted shore.

In our four years of living in Alaska, this physical beauty never became commonplace. The rain, that got old, but the mountains, veined with snow and rooted in the sea, were a wonderfulness every day.

I looked to the west, where Chatham branches to divide Baranof from Chichagof Island at Peril Strait. Twenty miles north was Tenakee Springs, a tiny town that crowded a boardwalk and climbed the hillside. A few Juneau residents had weekend cabins there and one, an artist, was especially known for her playful scenes of Tenakee's public baths and colorful little houses on stilts. Across the strait, on Admiralty Island, the Native village of Angoon guarded the entrance to Kootznahoo Inlet. There the houses, weathered and unpainted, rose from the beach as if in a perpetual state of siege; the artist who created *Raven Woman* lived in one of them. Remembering that picture, I thought of the woman's face, her steady, far-off gaze, her mouth and forehead and jaw. Everything about her was in complete repose and at the same time fully alert. She seemed ready to spring into action, right out of the frame, or lean back against the raven behind her. The raven was a looming presence, feathers ragged and shoulders hunched, but its dark eye was as quiet and knowing as the woman's. Connecting them—one of those details that had been there all along but that I'd never thought about before—was a splay of gray green and black green leaves, knotted and tangled and alive, fusing raven and woman together. Colors of the wilderness, here in this latitude, in this light.

Neither Tenakee nor Angoon was visible now, nor were they likely to be when we sailed past. Here and there a navigation marker, here and there a fishing boat, here and there a sailboat racing. Overwhelmingly the mountains, the low gray ceiling of the sky, and the surface of the sea.

I WAS SUDDENLY, COMPLETELY, exhausted. The past couple of hours had required hard work and attention, but I was also feeling an unaccustomed detachment from everything around me. I tried to shake my vision clear when I looked at the chart but I couldn't read the tiny print. Was I that tired? Of course: The patch.

I'd had it on since morning, not wanting seasickness to catch me. Predictably, it had dried my mouth, something I ignored; in these seas better a dry mouth, I reasoned, than multiple trips forward to the head, which would have been necessary if I'd been drinking lots of water. And the taste—it was as if all I could taste was my tongue, or the sloughing cells of my own body. There was no life for me in the soup-and-sandwich dinner Larry served us.

Now something else was happening. I'd catch myself staring too long at the way the strands of line were braided, red and white, or the pattern of salt spray on the fairlead blocks, or the streaks of foam on the backside of each wave. Trivial details mesmerized me. Whatever was causing all this, the scopolamine patch wasn't helping. I'd read those warnings on the package about blurred vision and impaired judgment when operating heavy machinery—a category that certainly included *Eagle*. Better to risk a little nausea than keep on this course.

I peeled the patch off my neck and rolled it into a ball.

What would definitely help was sleep, and it was time to kick in the watch routine anyway. Ours began at midnight, and though it was barely six o'clock, I was ready to sleep until then. Funny how relaxed I felt on *Eagle* now, after that disorienting accidental jibe. It was the same sea, a little rougher in fact, and conditions could worsen further. It was the same crew, and any one of us could make a mistake. Yet I felt safe.

The hull hummed through the water, the rigging hummed through the air. Stretched in my berth, the lee cloth holding me in like a crib rail, I let myself breathe deeply. I could hear Tim and Larry arrange themselves in their own berths. Beneath and around me *Eagle* lifted and sank, and when she sank it was like a bough dropping down and down, then swinging up again after a soft, weightless pause. The sea was an enormous, breathing belly and I a cat stretched upon it, purring.

IN MY DEEPEST SLEEP, I was awakened. "The wind's dropped," Tim said, standing above me in the darkness. My eyes opened instantly at the sound of his voice. "They need us out there to reset the spinnaker."

Without thinking, I sat up and pulled wool trousers over my long underwear, jammed on my boots. "Almost time for our watch anyway," Tim added; he and Larry were already zipping up their jackets. Hurrying to catch up, I lost myself momentarily in the tunnels of my sweater. *God, but I'm not a night person.*

It was an eerie midnight, gray and cottony. Against the black bulk of Baranof Island I could see the tiny masthead lights of the fleet. Tim and Steve—they were so *awake*—identified the boats that were closest. "All the spinnakers came down after you guys went below," Frank announced proudly; we hadn't reduced sail too early after all. "We're making good time."

Eagle was no longer charging northward, rising and falling. The cresting sea that had rushed us along was now a washboard, flecked with the suds of whitecaps. Half awake, I handled the main sheet from the cockpit as we jibed, repeating automatically yesterday's motions. I could hear Tim at the bow, directing Larry and Mike as they raised the spinnaker. They hunched over their work in the gloom, their angular forms rounded with the padding of wool caps and insulated jackets.

The huge sail inflated and for a moment *Eagle* resisted the tug of a thousand square feet of translucent, airborne nylon. Then a sound like a huge sigh and she surrendered to a new, faster pace.

Tim wanted four people on deck while we were racing with spinnaker, and Steve volunteered to stay up with us. "I don't need much sleep," he said, clearly energized by the way the race was going. "I'll catch some later." His eyes, like Tim's, were bright and alert. Larry's were more like mine— soft and slightly out of focus, as if still dreaming.

Mike went below, and Frank went soon after. "I'll be up to relieve you in a while," he said to Steve. As long as we had spinnaker conditions, the off-watch would alternate every two hours: first Steve, then Frank, then Mike; Tim, Larry, and I after that. I nodded at this new arrangement, though I could barely follow the logic.

The gurgling wake became an accustomed sound, like a quiet motor. Sailing is never silent. Dacron quivers in the wind, lines slap the deck and masts, fittings creak. The water is a dull rush. Sometimes the propeller vibrates. Every sound tells a story about wind, water, and speed. You sail with your ears as much as your eyes.

All these sounds, and *Eagle*'s own liveliness, soon roused me. It was gratifying to be racing, even pulling ahead at

times. When Tim or Steve directed us to make changes—
me on the main, Larry on the spinnaker—we were usually rewarded with improved performance. Tim, intent
on everything, nevertheless seemed relaxed at the wheel,
as if standing in the cold in the middle of the night, in a
cockpit little bigger than a bathtub, was a pure, private joy.
He gave me the briefest smile when he saw I was watching
him, as if he'd been caught having too much fun. I looked
away, watched the masthead lights moving north with us;
it was reassuring to see the others in relation to us. The
feel of competing against and *with* the fleet—I was struck
again by the sense of belonging to something in motion,
going forward with a life of its own.

"Did Frank tell you *Airloom*'s catching up?" Steve asked.
He shook his head, as if he couldn't believe it yet wanted
to. "There's a reason for those long keels." It was the first
time I'd heard him speak so admiringly about another
boat; in fact, he'd hardly referred to any of the boats we
were racing, other than *Silver Girl* the other night, or, ironi-
cally enough, his comment on *Airloom*'s cluttered rig at the
start three days ago. Or was it four? Steve seemed to keep
his attention on *Eagle,* as if all that mattered in this race
was the boat he was sailing and the conditions of water
and air around her. He noted whatever was happening on
the other side of Chatham Strait—or even five hundred
feet away—of course, but how another boat might steer or
set a sail didn't determine what he did.

In this race each boat was so different anyway. Beneath
me, *Eagle*'s fin keel and spade rudder sliced through the
water, her hull, as gently curved as the fuselage of a jet,

gliding at the surface. I pictured *Airloom*'s deeper hull, her rounded, buoyant belly, the way her keel ran almost the full length of her, like *Orca*'s—built to track long distances in heavy seas. Green water could wash her deck to the gunwales and she'd shake it off without a pause. Sluggish in light air but reassuring and responsive when things got rough.

I tried to picture the crew. As light as the wind had been those first days of the race, and as poky as *Airloom* was in those conditions, they hadn't dropped out. Like we had. What had kept them racing? Why hadn't they turned on their engine and joined the rest of us in Warm Springs Bay? Instead, they'd sailed on with only a brief rest. They knew they couldn't win, that they'd place last, yet they continued. Behind but still racing, *Airloom* was more inspiring than *Silver Girl*, now far, far ahead.

Larry and I had taken our positions midship on the port rail. I hugged my knees. It seemed that we were softly rocking in place, everything else gliding swiftly by. It was too early for sunrise, but already the sky was releasing a pale light that nudged the dimness aside, into the forests. That was an illusion too, that the sun rose. It was we who were moving, five men and one woman moving over *Eagle*, *Eagle* propelled by air over water, the water and air moving over the earth, the earth spinning so that the tiny space we occupied was turning toward the sun. Yet the illusion of that fixed star moving instead remained.

Last night's blow had scoured everything: the aluminum sky, the serrated islands, even the sea. The only softness was a sash of cloud wrapped loosely around every mountain.

Admiralty Island was a tall shadow at my back. We had been circling the island forever, it seemed, and its silent bulk had taken on the character of a continent, or a planet. A large bird flew eastward: black, wedge shaped, tail fanned—a raven or an eagle, I couldn't tell for sure, though *it* could make out every detail on this boat if it wanted to. There was more to a bird's-eye view than a simple change of perspective; it saw with different eyes. If I could rise from *Eagle* to fly with it across Admiralty, acres of forest and muskeg would pass beneath me, lakes, rivers, mountains with their own small glaciers, inlets whose jade-colored water was as transparent as glass. Like a planet, the island just *was,* complete and perfect by itself, belonging to no one: not the miners who periodically boomed and busted, not the hunters or hikers. Not even those who lived in the cabins and houses that faced outward from the ribbon of beach, as if yearning to be waterborne.

Icy Strait opened to the west; fifty miles beyond was Cross Sound and the whole wide ocean. Only two hundred years ago—an eye blink in geologic time—the strait had been studded with icebergs calved from the frozen rivers that had formed Glacier Bay. Now *there* was a place that made me feel insignificant. Paul and I had anchored once way up the east arm, where the glaciers had retreated within our lifetime, which is to say recently. Yesterday. The earth was bare and new, and the air cold and odorless. We'd had to retreat into the cabin after a while, overwhelmed by the landscape. It was like anchoring on the moon.

I shivered, as if the retreating glaciers had left their chill ghosts behind to wander on Icy Strait. I pulled my wool cap closer around my ears and wiped my dripping nose with the back of my gloved hand. Looking south, I watched the red and green running lights of a fishing boat grow brighter and closer. Its trawling poles were erect and its black hull seemed to be pushing a white ruffle with its bow. Inside the pilothouse the skipper would be warm; there would be a pot of coffee on the console, I imagined, and from below the heavy diesel would rumble on and on.

I loved the look of vessels like that: all business, built for strength, more valued for their experience than their appearance. And their crews were so eclectic; there was no way to tell who they were. Living here, I'd soon learned that most had other jobs—they had to, to make a living, since fishing could be lucrative but usually wasn't. So the men and women in that shapeless rain gear were also engineers, bank tellers, electricians.

Janet, the woman who cut my hair in Seattle, was married to one of them. Her husband, a teacher, spent his summer fishing out of Sitka.

"Every summer? All summer?"

"It's great for him," she said, snipping with her tiny scissors. "I miss him, but he comes back with so much energy."

I could hardly imagine an entire summer separated from Paul. The one time we'd lived apart, while he worked in Seattle and I stayed behind in Juneau to get *Orca* ready for the trip south, we got so out of synch that it took months before our lives meshed together again. Like splicing a three-strand line: It's so simple to do, but when you're out of practice tucking that last strand seems impossible, and keeping even tension on all the strands is hard too. How did their marriage survive?

"It's good for us. We write. Letters. Lots of them." She combed back my straight brown hair, looked closely for wisps. "And we communicate in a whole different way. Some of our best conversations take place in those letters."

"Does it make a difference the rest of the year?"

"Oh yes. In fact we've just started writing stories to each other. You know those cards you can buy that are blank inside? We write a short story inside, based on the picture."

I smiled at her reflection in the mirror as she dried my hair. Here was this flourishing old-fashioned romance, a *correspondence,* in the true sense of the word.

She gave my hair a final comb and pulled off my cape. "And to think I worried that our marriage wouldn't go anywhere after a while. Just freeze up into nothing but trips to the mall."

That could be him, I thought, watching from *Eagle* as the trawler headed out toward Cross Sound. What story was he writing now?

"POINT COUVERDEN," SAID TIM, pointing northwest. We were approaching the red buoy that marked Hanus Reef, in the middle of the entrance to Icy Strait. The buoy seemed to mark nothing, but a reef was there, submerged. Three miles beyond, a red light flashed against the dark shore. Paul and I had often navigated *Orca* on a course through the islands there to the refuge of Swanson Harbor.

Like Taku Harbor on the other side of Admiralty
Island, like Warm Springs Bay to the south, Swanson was
a favorite anchorage: protection from gales, the perfect
depth for anchoring, perfect mud for an anchor to grip.
A halfway point between Juneau and Glacier Bay, with
a sturdy wooden float detached from the islands, like a
raft—some said to discourage curious bears. Busy with
cruisers from Down South all summer but a remote, wild
place in early spring and late fall. And the crabbing! We
could limit out every time, huge male Dungeness I gut-
ted and split immediately, which turned red-orange in my
boiling pot.

We'd had good times among those islands—there were
stories to tell—yet I said nothing to Tim, Larry, or Steve.
Since the start of this second leg we'd done little chatting.
Each of us seemed to have retreated inward, thinking our
private thoughts in a silence that was nevertheless com-
panionable. Separate, but tuned to one another. I liked the
feeling, though there seemed to be no word for it. The way
an animal feels, perhaps: a deer browsing, then raising its
head to stare into the middle distance, relaxed and atten-
tive. I felt ready to respond, alert to what was happening
yet without anxiety about what *might* happen next, as if balanced between knowing everything and knowing nothing.

I wanted this feeling to last, as I wanted the southerly
that was blowing us so beautifully across Icy Strait to last.

The light off Point Couverden blinked—one second,
two seconds, three seconds, four seconds—and blinked
again. "Fl 4sec" it would say on the chart, right next to a
fat, purple exclamation mark. Under way, Paul and I were

forever deciphering these symbols. It was the only way
to know what was beneath the surface, and at times what
was on the surface but obscured. Those blue lines on a
chart that swirl like watermarks on taffeta? They indicate
depth. Lines that connect like veins on a leaf indicate
prop-snagging kelp. Scallops mean reefs, and tiny crosses
and stars are unforgiving rocks. When they're circled by a
dotted line—so faint you could easily dismiss it—the rock
is especially dangerous.

"Just go where there aren't any rocks," a ferryboat captain quipped, but it isn't that easy unless you only cruise
in familiar waters, and not even then. Paul and I weren't
twenty-five miles from Seattle and I was steering *Orca*
around a point I'd navigated many times when the sound
thunk! thunk! moved through her hull right into my feet and
up to my heart. Paul was out the hatch and on deck in an
instant. We looked around, saw nothing, and knew we'd
hit something hard. So while I kept *Orca* into the wind in
a sort of stall, Paul tore up every hatch, looking for water
that might be filling the bilges. Not a drop. We anchored
as soon as we could, and Paul dove below in his wet suit.
He surfaced a few minutes later to breathlessly spit out
the words, "She's okay. Just a chunk. In the forefoot. Barely
nicked."

Naturally, the rock was charted. I'd seen it—a single
cross blurred by a circle of dots—but hadn't paid attention to the tide or our distance from shore. Had I known
exactly *where* I was and *when* I was, which I should have,
exactly, I wouldn't have hit that rock.

Paul claimed he should have been paying attention too,

which made it easier for me to forgive myself. We wrote "Orca's Rock" in prominent letters on our chart. We knew we'd been lucky. We also knew the joke about the two kinds of liars: those who claim they've never run aground and those who claim they never will again.

Eagle, and all of the fleet that I could see, stayed well east of the Hanus Reef buoy. In another hour we would slip past Swanson Harbor, where boats were anchored now in silence, their sleeping crews oblivious to the race passing by.

Somewhere in that labyrinth of islands and channels was the charted reef that Herm and Joyce had hit in *Athena.* I sighed to myself, remembering their story and missing Joyce all over again. It was their second night out of Juneau, the very beginning of the voyage that would eventually take them to Mexico. They'd been at anchor when the williwaws hit—those screaming, intermittent winds that drop from the mountains without warning. *Athena* dragged onto the reef as the tide was going out. Their distress call was heard—talk about luck—by a Coast Guard training vessel nearby, which dispatched a small boat with large pumps and three eager young men. But neither the pumps nor the men were needed. *Athena* had not been impaled, only punched and bruised, and she righted herself without flooding when the tide rose. A day of fiberglass repair at the dock in Hoonah, the Native village across Icy Strait, and Herm and Joyce were on their way. They never considered calling off the voyage, or even postponing it.

"We should have known the instant *Athena* stayed sideways to the wind that she was dragging anchor," Herm explained when they told us the story months later in Seattle. "We should have moved faster."

"We'd spent so much time getting ready to *leave*," Joyce added. "All that preparing and we'd forgotten what cruising really was—sailing, motoring, anchoring. Always paying attention."

Inevitably, sailing skiffs will capsize. Large boats will run aground. You could be cruising along, laughing, or snug in your berth, and a slight change in course, the push of wind or current, a moment's inattention, and your keel grazes a rock, or hits it hard. Or passes by without a sound, missing it by a foot or a fathom.

And if you go nowhere, tie your boat to a dock or tether it to the bottom on a chain? Little by little lines chafe, anchors drag.

I RUBBED MY EYES and scratched my scalp under the itchy wool cap. We were almost abeam of the Couverden light. The sky was the lightest yellow, the softest gray, though it couldn't be sunrise yet. I'd done pretty well staying awake so far, but the hypnotic hiss of *Eagle*'s wake and her gentle rocking motion were getting to me. There hadn't been much activity for Larry or me in the last hour. In this steady following wind, *Eagle* seemed to be sailing herself.

Frank appeared in the hatch and was passing mugs of hot chocolate to the four of us on deck. Only two o'clock, I thought, and he looked more awake than I felt.

"Ready for a break?" he asked Steve.

Steve shook his head. "I'm fine. In these conditions,

I'm probably good to the end." Tim nodded; so was he. So
was Larry.

"Go below if you like, Migael," Frank said. "You look
like you could use some more sleep. We'll call you up later."

I didn't protest. "Thanks," I said. Though I'd been
determined to make it through this watch, I was mighty
relieved that I didn't have to. I didn't even have to pretend
I could, thanks to Steve's reserves of strength, if that's
what he was calling on; maybe he just didn't need much
sleep. Maybe strength or weakness had nothing to do with
it. Certainly no one else was using those words.

Anticipating the coziness of my sleeping bag and the
marvelous sensation of stretching out horizontally, I sipped
the hot chocolate. It *tasted*. God, but I was glad I'd taken off
that patch. It tasted sweet and rich, and its warmth spread
from my stomach to all my limbs.

SUNLIGHT ENTERED *EAGLE*'S CABIN as it does
Orca's, indirectly, refracted off the water in golden streaks
that flickered over the teak bulkheads and in white dap-
ples that danced on the overhead. I was up in an instant,
fully rested, eager to be outside in the brightness.

"Good morning," Tim said in a voice so welcoming I
had an impulse to hug him. He and Steve seemed not to
have moved from the cockpit since I'd gone below. Mike,
who looked as refreshed as I now felt, waved from the foredeck where he was sitting next to Larry. Frank, apparently,
had gone back to his berth sometime when I was asleep.

"Give me one hour at most," Steve said to Tim when he

saw me. "If I'm not up, wake me." I stepped aside and he
was down the companionway ladder.

"What time is it?" I asked, suddenly mortified that I
might have overslept.

Tim looked at his watch. "Not quite six." Four hours;
no wonder I felt like I'd slept all night—I practically had.
"Mike just got up himself," Tim continued. "We've been
spelling each other okay. The wind's fallen off and we
figured everyone might as well get the sleep they need.
It hasn't been a problem. Besides, we're almost there."

I turned around to see what he was seeing. There it
was—Point Retreat—the northernmost tip of Admiralty
Island. Our final turn in the race. The finish at the south
end of Shelter Island was less than ten miles away.

The sea was rippled, the breeze light but steady from
the south, still filling the spinnaker and the mainsail,
which stood like a great white wing nearly perpendicular to *Eagle*'s deck. The rest of the fleet was about equally
divided ahead of and behind us; we were all slowly con-
verging, homing in toward Point Retreat like birds, our
brightly colored spinnakers thrust forward. Above us, the
cool air so magnified the mountains that in every direction
they seemed to have moved up into the sky, their sharp
edges honed by the light. North, where Chatham Strait
narrowed to become Lynn Canal, the even steeper mountains looked like one continuous jagged wall. The sun,
already warm on my face, gilded everything.

I don't know where the next hour went, what was said
or even what I thought of. I must have made adjustments
to the main, and Mike and Larry to the spinnaker. Tim's

hands were delicate on the wheel, barely moving but never still. What I did that hour was mostly watch Point Retreat grow larger.

Channel fever had set in—at least that's what Paul and I called it, that affliction that so mesmerizes us when we're almost home. Part exhilaration, part longing, with a tinge of sadness that the voyage is coming to an end. Everything else falls away, even hunger when I should be hungry, exhaustion when I should feel tired. The past and the future stand aside, for though I'm fixed on the end—I can't help it; I'm moving toward it inevitably and there's no turning back—my attention is entirely on the present moment, the movement through it to the next moment, and to the one after that.

I didn't know if the others were feeling as I was, though their silence and faraway gazes told me they were. We weren't waiting through time so much as watching it. Of course we were racing, trying to sail swiftly and efficiently, but the sensation wasn't hurried. With the wind at our backs *Eagle*'s progress seemed effortless. Moment by moment, the sky, the sea, the shoreline changed, and the moments themselves were palpable, as if time had breadth and weight.

Then Frank stepped on deck, and then Steve, and we were a full crew again.

"Prepare to sheet in the main," Steve said when we were almost abeam of the Point Retreat light. Tim stepped aside to give him the helm. "Larry. Mike. Stand by the spinnaker." I scooted aft, they scooted forward, and Tim joined them.

Steve turned the wheel to starboard as Frank and I

slowly brought in the main, with sheet and traveler, to capture the wind that was now abeam. There was a great deal happening on the bow that I didn't try to follow as the spinnaker swung to port: adjustments at the pole and the mast, and in the cockpit, adjustments to the sheets.

"Right *there,*" Steve said, and instantly lines were cleated off, neatly and rapidly coiled.

Eagle rounded the point and seemed about to accelerate, but slowed to a creep instead. The long, towering mass of Admiralty Island had stolen the southerly wind. Ahead, barely moving, were the boats that had outraced us. Every one, even *Silver Girl.*

"Douse that spinnaker," Steve ordered. "And be careful how you move!" Down came the parachute of red, white, and blue nylon, weightless as a cloud. Up went our largest genoa, tethered with our lightest sheet lines. No lurching, no fumbling. Barely any talk. *Eagle* slipped through the glassy water.

"Now look," Steve said, hands hovering over the wheel. His voice was calm, but his eyes were eager, as though the sight of all those boats ahead of us had charged him. "This is where everything we've learned can really pay off." Tim and Frank nodded in complete, enthusiastic agreement. "Migael, you're the lightest. You handle the genoa sheet here in the cockpit. Tim, stay aft with us on the main sheet. Everybody else forward on the starboard side. We've got to keep this baby level."

What wind we had—there was the barest breeze, aloft above our heads—came off our starboard. And on this wind we coasted: southeast past Barlow Point, where a

lone whale breathed as if asleep in the silver water; east
toward Shelter Island, where one by one the boats ahead
of us ghosted to the finish. Beyond was the white mass of
the Mendenhall Glacier, its curved descent striped gray
and black, like a highway from the icefields. A magnet
pulling us on.

Just ahead, no more than a boat length, was *Casa Mía*.
Her sails were set as *Eagle*'s were, her crew positioned
almost the same as well. We'd been behind her since noon
yesterday, when we'd had to make those two full circles
for barging at the start, and we'd dropped our spinnaker
earlier too. To see *Casa Mía*'s stern this close—we'd done
well to have caught up like this.

"It's a steak dinner if you can beat *Casa Mía*," Frank said
from the bow.

Steve didn't respond directly but something about him
changed, the set of his shoulders perhaps, the muscles in his
jaw; somehow he seemed both tighter and looser. He cen-
tered the bill of his Eagle cap—the sun was bright and we
all had ours on by now—and I noticed Tim push his slightly
back. There was no reading the expression in anyone's eyes
through our dark glasses, but it was clear that we'd taken
Frank's challenge.

Steve suggested an adjustment or two at the bow. He
glanced at me and dropped his voice to a whisper.

"Sheet in," he said. I cranked the winch slowly, a click at
a time. "That's right. Hold it." A pause of no more than a
second. "Sheet out"—I held the line with my left hand and
eased out the wraps with the palm of my right—". . . slowly.
In now." The softest whisper, as if he were talking to

himself, a whisper I'd no more expected than I'd expected
to be assigned to the cockpit at such a critical time, handling the genoa sheet.

In, then out, in again. It was like sailing a little dinghy,
light on the water, adjusting the sail second by second to
the perfect curve, the most efficient airfoil. I squinted up
at *Eagle*'s genoa, tried to see what Steve saw—the barest
luffing at the head of the sail, a flutter in the leech, a sag in
the sheet—but before I could think what to do Steve had
already corrected it. "In . . . that's it."

I lost track of time, of place, of everything but the winch
and the line in my hand. Now and then I looked across
the cockpit at Tim who, responding to his own signals,
as continuously and minutely adjusted the main. I never
turned around to look at Steve, who stood at my back. I was
an extension of *Eagle* and her crew, and the six of us seemed
to exist only to help her capture every breath of wind, every
thermal of moving air. She glided on, never stalling.

Twice we caught up to *Casa Mía*. Twice her sails blanketed ours. Then we were nose to nose, not twenty feet
apart. The briefest glance at the crew; I heard their voices
and the jewel-like clicks of *Casa Mía*'s winches, but my ears
were tuned to Steve's whispered commands: "Out . . . a bit
more . . ."

So intent was I on my tiny part in *Eagle*'s progress that
the finish buoy took me by surprise. It seemed to material-
ize in front of us. Just then, a puff—the slightest breeze—
filled our genoa. *Eagle*'s bow inched past *Casa Mía*'s to the
finish.

We exploded into groans and laughter, threw our arms

wide. Mike and Larry were up now, standing on the bow, and Frank was all but dancing. Tim kept smiling at him, then at Steve, then at the rest of us, then at Frank again.

Skill, I thought, feeling accomplished. *We did it after all.*

"Luck," Steve said aloud, as if he had read my mind. "Dumb luck."

THE SAILS WERE DOWN before I could catch my breath. The engine was on. The race was over.

I'd expected some finishing ceremony or remarks, the pop of a champagne cork or at least the announcement of a fresh pot of coffee. But the end was as quiet as the beginning had been in Juneau harbor five days ago, as if racing was no different from any other activity. Frank, Steve, and Mike went below to sleep; their watch had been the most disrupted last night and the excitement of nosing past *Casa Mía* seemed to have drained the last of their energy.

With Tim at the helm, Larry and I untangled what seemed like miles of line and acres of sail. We coiled, furled, folded, and stowed—all for the last time. The decks and cockpit looked naked when we were done.

Tim pointed *Eagle* southeast and we began the six hours of motoring that would take us around the west side of Douglas Island and back into Juneau. "I'd like to get in a few winks," he said after Larry went below to make lunch. "Will you take the helm for a while?"

"Sure!" I felt as if the day was starting, not ending. No small thanks to everyone who let me sleep last night. I was hungry too—ravenous actually. When had we last eaten? All I could remember was hot chocolate, a few cookies.

I took the wheel. The chrome was smooth and warm
and I realized with a start that this was the first time I
had touched it. Immediately and instinctively my stance
widened, my field of vision expanded. Something inside
me shifted.

"Could I see the chart?" I asked. Tim reached down
through the hatch and handed me a chart that was neatly
quarter-folded to the northwest shore of Douglas Island.
I ticked off the landmarks and hazards: There's George
Rock, a scattering of rocks and shoals north and west off
Douglas—keep all that well to port. There's Colt Island
and Horse Island off Admiralty, with shoals to the east—
favor Douglas through there, and as soon as Point Hilda's
visible, head closer. I put the chart on the bench beside
me, weighing it down with a winch handle. "Thanks. I
think I've got it."

Tim yawned broadly, stretched out on the cockpit
bench and covered his face with his cap. His ears were
bright red and I touched the tops of mine, felt the sunburn there. I had forgotten to use sunscreen this morning. Come to think of it, I'd forgotten about everything
except racing. For the past couple of hours my world had
condensed down to nothing more than this small boat,
thirty-four feet long, six feet of fin keel below, forty-eight
feet of mast above. Everything else had been backdrop
and supporting cast. Even myself. Even the extraordinary
mountains, the dazzling blue water.

I looked over my shoulder—almost too late—and
watched the Mendenhall Glacier disappear behind Outer
Point.

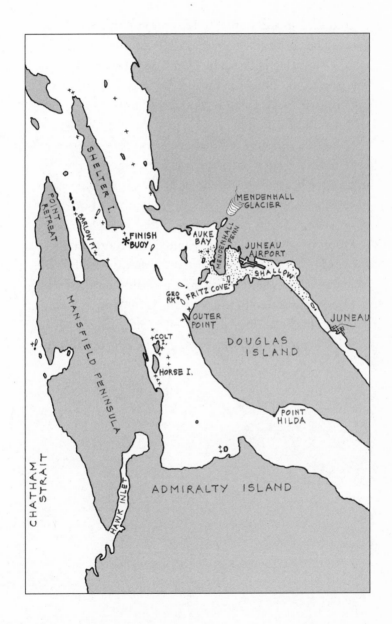

I looked ahead. I breathed deeply and smiled. It was great to be at the wheel, in the center of the cockpit, the engine vibrating beneath my feet, *Eagle*'s bow parting the water in front of me. I knew the race was over, but steering now with such pleasure I imagined myself on a voyage that was just beginning.

And that's when I remembered—no, *saw*—the twelve-year-old girl I once was, caught in a snapshot. My mother must have been off to the side, for the black-and-white photo she took captured us in profile on the shore: my older sisters, hands on their hips with the slightly bored postures of adolescence; my younger brothers leaning forward in excitement, the little one smothered in a life jacket; my father in his midforties probably—my age now—bent over a wooden pram, readying it for launch. I am standing in the middle of the photo, flat chest out, shoulders back, proudly holding the oars. Looking out to sea.

FINISHING LINES

"I DON'T KNOW WHERE to start," I said in answer
to Paul's question. The phone connection was so clear that
his voice made me giddy and his presence was something I
could physically feel, the way I was still feeling *Eagle*'s rocking motion even though I was firmly aground.

"Well, I take it you didn't win."

"Not by a long shot," I said, laughing. My voice sounded
a bit hoarse but our talking felt easy; the enforced pauses
of the satellite delay seemed more like a rhythm we were
taking in stride than an interruption. "Didn't even finish
the first leg, but that's a story in itself." I thought back to
the tension that had lingered around that decision. We
had been a different crew then. "The guys were great, the
weather couldn't have been better—only one real blow."

"You sound tired."

"You know, I am. Beat." I'd been at the wheel most
of the afternoon, and while there was absolutely nothing
arduous about the run back to Juneau around Douglas
Island—the steady sound of the motor, the breeze on my
face, the glare of the sun on the water—those hours had

tired me as surely as if I had walked the twenty-odd miles, pulling *Eagle* behind me like a cart.

But good tired. I'd liked all that time steering while the others napped off and on for as long as they wanted. I felt like I was paying back the favor they'd extended to me the night before, when I'd been left to sleep for so many hours undisturbed. And when we were northbound at last, less than an hour out of Juneau, and everyone was on deck—even Steve, who not surprisingly had slept all afternoon—no one remarked on any of this, and I liked that too.

"I'll take it from here," Tim had said, and from then on he, Frank, and Larry handled everything. *Eagle* seemed to turn into the marina on her own, nose into her slip, secure her own lines.

"Anyway," I said to Paul, sighing, almost yawning. "I should sleep well tonight." With very little encouragement I could fall onto Tim and Stella's hide-a-bed right now, though the sun still reflected off a patch of snow on the top of Mount Roberts and the sky was far from dark. After a long, hot shower and a complete change of clothes, that is, and the meal I could hear Stella preparing. "But I wanted to call you as soon as we got in. See how you're doing."

A pause, longer than the satellite delay. "Not so good." His answer was quiet, like an intake of breath. Another pause, as if he were turning over in his head whether to say more and how to say it. I waited, knowing that if I spoke my transmission would either cover his words or stop them altogether.

And then it all came out. Everything at the house was

behind schedule. The exterior walls had been closed in
only two days ago. The plumbing and wiring were far from
done. Okay, delays were normal, but without consulting
him the contractor had invited his kids up, and then his
parents, and on and off his wife, who was still his wife,
Paul guessed, though we'd understood they were getting a
divorce. The whole family had been camping in the yard,
lounging on the beach.

"It's like the work *stopped*," Paul explained. "When I
suggested that this was a job, not a vacation, he looked
hurt. Said he was running into too many problems with
the way the house had been built in the first place." I knew
Paul was thinking of his dad, who'd built the house with
used materials mostly, and in his spare time, learning as
he went. There'd been no money to do it "right" or to hire
so much as a ditch digger. How could there be, with four
children and a wife to support? Yet he and Paul's mom
had managed to turn a beach cabin into a home, and the
implied criticism of their efforts seemed petty and wrong.

"So I've taken over some of the work," Paul said. And
as he explained how he was pulling wire, hanging doors,
running pipe, and pounding studs—doing everything he
could, in short, to keep the project moving—I felt my chest
expanding. He was being taken advantage of, clearly, by
someone we were paying well and by the hour. Sure, Paul
was an architect; he could manage projects and keep things
pretty much on schedule for his own clients. But for him
to do it for himself was another matter. And he'd made the
classic mistake—I had too—of treating the person we'd
hired as a friend. Now that "friend" was beginning to drag

his feet on the business deal that was, in reality, the basis
for our relationship.

All this came to me with complete clarity, as if what
Paul was going through could have been predicted, though
not avoided. And what was also clear was that I would
never have seen this if I were there with him, in the middle
of it all.

"How's your mom taking this?" I asked. Like Paul, she
saw the world with optimistic eyes. She wasn't used to
being tricked or used.

"She keeps saying not to worry on her account, but
I can tell she's disappointed. She wants back into the
house." Which was originally planned for two weeks from
now; at this rate we'd be lucky if the house was ready in
two months.

I was about to lash out—at the delays, the contractor,
the entire project gone bad. But just then I thought of
that night on the east side of Prince of Wales Island. It
was our last night in Alaska waters, and all day we'd been
sailing under fair skies that seduced us into going farther
than, in hindsight, we should have. By the time we turned
into the nearest anchorage that looked good on the chart,
the protected coves had already been taken by fishing
boats. It was dark by the time we found a bay with anchoring room, and then the wind came up, or rather not *up* but
down the steep mountains, williwaws that fought against us
as we tried to set the hook three times, and twice Paul had
to crank up over two hundred feet of chain by hand, with
me at the wheel working the throttle to resist the hard
blasts. Still we couldn't trust the anchor but stayed awake

until the wind died, which it did as suddenly as it had
begun, as such wind always dies. And awake we'd talked:
This is crazy, risking everything we own. When we get to
Seattle we'll sell *Orca,* buy a house or a condo like everyone
else, lead an ordinary, safe life. But in the morning the
sun was warm and the bay was a mirror, and even Dixon
Entrance was calm. We motored all the way across into
Canada, amused at our talk the night before.

"If I can change my ticket, I'm coming home Saturday,"
I said abruptly into the phone. I felt suddenly, irrationally
strong, ready to take on an army of builders, though I'd
been exhausted when I called. "And you don't need to pick
me up at the airport. I'll take the shuttle into town, no
problem, and drive up Sunday morning." I was talking fast,
a rush of plans.

"That would be great." Paul's voice was a relieved
exhale. "I know we had other plans but—that would be
great." I pictured him standing right now in the stripped-
out kitchen, tool belt hanging on his hips, tired and overwhelmed but utterly focused. He had another week of
leave from his job and he would work on the house every
waking minute, and every spare minute afterward. He'd
finish that house by himself if that was what it took.

So much for my fantasy homecoming: Paul at the
airport when my plane landed, a quiet evening on *Orca,*
talking over dinner about our—to be honest, mostly
my—experiences since we parted, a renewing sleep after
lovemaking. I regretted letting the fantasy go, but only a
little. The past week had been all sail and wind and motion, had seemed a voyage away from everything, but like

all circumnavigations it had ended exactly where it began. Paul, who had stayed behind, had been moving forward, or at least trying to, day by day, and there was nothing for it now but to join him, jump back in, look around for the right tools, find a place in the swirling action. With luck, that would be in two more days.

"You're sure you'll be okay?" His question was heartfelt, and I knew what he meant: Would I be okay alone through the night? Was it all right for him not to be there with me, to let go a little? In his question I felt the love behind that care, the weight of it, and what it had cost him.

"Yes," I answered, with a certainty that surprised me. "I'll be fine. You need to stay where you are." I couldn't explain how being alone on *Orca* wouldn't make me afraid, and even if it did *being* afraid wasn't important, what mattered was something bigger. How could I explain what I didn't understand myself? You wait for the tide to come in, you stare and stare and nothing seems to change. But turn away for a while and when you look back things are different. Rocks on shore that were dull and gray are jade and amethyst and ebony. Barnacles that were brittle and closed are feathery and alive.

"It'll help so much to have you here," Paul said. "To have your help." I knew that somehow he had followed my thoughts, long distance, just as I knew what he was saying beneath his words: Thanks for coming back. Thanks for being able to help, and for wanting to.

SOLID. UNMOVING. STRANGE. *I'm on land now,* I reminded myself as I woke. I sat up in the hide-a-bed, closed my eyes and opened them again. The mountains across the channel lurched slightly, then held still. I put one bare foot on the floor, expecting it to tilt. I put down the other foot. When I stood up, nothing swayed.

The house was quiet, as only an empty house can be, and the morning sky was overcast and shadowless, with no color at all. A relief, really—less seemed to be expected of me. I'd already overslept, and the note Tim and Stella had left on the breakfast table said to help myself to anything in the refrigerator, and to please feel free to use the car. Typical Alaskan hospitality: your every need taken care of, including the need to be on your own.

Outside, the cool air soothed my sunburned face. The long climb up the stairs from the house to the road stretched my calves and hamstrings and seemed to reorder every vertebrae in my back. I could sure use a walk. Not downtown though; this was a day I wanted to myself for a while, after so much close living on *Eagle*. In town I'd inevitably run into someone I knew. Juneau was that kind of place, a city that was really a small town, where going to the post office or grocery store was a social event, not an errand.

So I headed to the valley instead, driving across the bridge I'd looked up at from *Eagle*'s deck not one week ago when the race began and not twelve hours ago when we returned. I turned left on Egan Drive, past Harris Harbor and Aurora Basin. The tide was in and I could look right across, instead of down, at the boats moored there. Then north, past the wetlands that made this end of Gastineau Channel look like a river now but that would

be an exposed marsh later, at low tide. The huge stump
was still out there, its trunk horizontal on a hump of sand,
one thick root arched upward, looking like a marooned
sea lion. A storm had blown it in years ago, and I remembered that Thanksgiving Day, how the wind had clocked
over ninety miles an hour, so much wind I couldn't walk
upright against it and *Orca's* lines had chafed halfway
through.

To the east, crowding the Old Glacier Highway, Mount
Juneau gave way to other steep mountains. *In spring the green
moves up,* I remembered, *in fall the white moves down.* Then the
Lemon Creek valley opened a vista that revealed part of
the icefield beyond. Before Heinzleman Ridge closed in,
I saw a swirl of birds hovering above the city landfill—gulls
circling, ravens tumbling, eagles soaring, all of them looking for something to scavenge or steal.

How easy it was to drive a car! Just step on the gas and
go. Step on the brake to slow down. Navigate by reading
the signs and following the lines in the road. No thought
of wind direction, tide, current, or at this time of year
worsening weather. No tacking back and forth to make
headway, no trimming or changing sails. The easiness went
to my head. And when I reached my destination, I simply
steered into a space between two painted lines, stopped,
shifted to Park, set the brake, and turned off the motor.

Not twenty minutes since I'd left the house, and I was
within a few miles of yesterday's finish line in Auke Bay.
But instead of water, islands, rocks, and headlands, everything moving and sinuous around me, I was in the middle
of a shopping mall, full of right angles and concrete. Not

the only mall here, either; I'd passed several on my way, but this one was only five miles or so from the Mendenhall Glacier. A little shopping for tonight's potluck, then a short hike, I was thinking. Do what I want, on my own. I could see the glacier from the parking lot, a dull ash-blue mass beyond the concrete and the cookie-cutter subdivisions, an arrested flow of ice held between pinnacle mountains. As I looked, the glacier seemed to grow larger and closer and to glow with a cold aqua light that pushed aside the low forest growing in the valley it had carved.

Something about its massiveness and blue-whiteness altered my mood. I hurried through my shopping, annoyed rather than inspired by the rows of packed, gaily colored boxes and cans. So much stuff, and it all seemed to demand one decision after another, though none were important. Even the flowers I bought for Stella only reminded me of the fireweed growing along the road I'd driven to get here, still bright pink but in less than a month it would begin turning white with seed and the summer that was never long enough would be over. The heady solstice time was already passing.

By the time I turned onto the Loop Road, I seemed to be driving to the glacier on instinct, giving in to a pull as powerful as current, for a reason I'd forgotten. Like the race, the course I was following was predetermined, and like the race I felt I had to complete it.

I caught my breath when I got out of the car at the visitors center. I'd been here many times, and every single time I was struck by the Mendenhall's dominating spirit. I know the glacier is an inanimate thing; gravity provides

the impetus for its journey from forty-five hundred feet
up in the icefield. But it *feels* alive. It exhales a frigid breath
as it crawls on its belly down between the mountains. It
poises its bulk at the edge of Mendenhall Lake and patiently
waits to calve. When an iceberg is born, the glacier moans
with a primitive rumble that is felt as powerfully as it is
heard, and can never be forgotten.

I turned off on a narrow path that descended to the lake
and sat on a smooth, round rock. A steady stream of tourists
moved like pilgrims along the boardwalk below me, toward
a sign that read Photo Point. They carried bright bags and
packs over their shoulders; many of them had cameras and
VCRs. A picture or two and they turned away. What would
they take back with them? What would I?

For a long while I stared at the frozen, undulating river,
letting its reality absorb all my thoughts. Comparisons
skittered uselessly down its icy walls like cobbles and were
swallowed into its crevasses: so heavy it crushes stone to
flour, so huge it seems to be always close. Ice so compressed
it absorbs all the colors of the spectrum but blue. The
Mendenhall's face alone is a mile and a half wide and two
hundred feet thick, the mouth of a river flowing so slowly
that a ride down the full twelve miles of its length, moving
at its pace, would take eighty years.

But the glacier that seemed so alive was also dying,
melting faster than its heavy advance. Since my first visit
only ten years ago it had retreated noticeably. The pile of
silt I once scaled in rubber boots was now a mere hump
of sand. The waterfall of Nugget Creek to the east, once
partially obscured by ice, was now fully visible. The bare

hill above it was green; grasses and shrubs had found root-room. Someday a forest will stand there.

Yet the glacier still seemed undiminished. Perhaps it was this stolidness, this permanence despite constant change, that I had come for. I tried to breathe these in with the thread of ice that was woven through the air like a scent. Knees up, fingers laced across them, I sat on the cold rock as though waiting for a sign.

All that came to me were thoughts of what was changed, or lost, and the memories were snapshots that I'd taken. Like the tourists at Photo Point, I'd posed my friends there too: A nephew, grown now, had grinned for my camera. A couple from Seattle, divorced now, had snuggled. Joyce and Herm had waved. By ones and twos they crowded into my field of vision, laughing, caught by my lens, and behind them the blue-white mass of ice. The shutter clicked and all of us were changed, some of us gone, and the glacier remained.

"After the first death, there is no other." What poet wrote that? Whoever he was, he was wrong. I'd lost others before Joyce—friends my age or a little older, a few younger. I didn't want to count them—there were too many lost to cancer. Faces turned to skulls, skin pressed like tissue paper against the bones, intelligent smiles gone to jaw and gum and teeth, eyes bright and alive and beyond rescue. Others, I knew, would follow, each a reminder of the death that preceded it, and of the one before that. I never got used to it and never would.

I briefly resisted the unwinding spool of these memories but they held me as surely as I was held sitting on

this rock. For days I had been afloat, racing; now all that
buoyant motion was beyond reach. I touched the hard
stone. My fingers traced the scars the Mendenhall had left
advancing—or was it retreating?—thousands of years ago.

It wasn't illness but accident that took another friend
when he fell from a cliff, and yet another years later when
his small plane crashed. And my grandfather Miguel when
the whirlwind hit, long before I was born. Sudden losses
without final good-byes, stretching behind and ahead.

And the near misses: They left scars too. That cancer
scare with Paul. In the weeks before his surgery we'd hardly
dared to speak the dread we felt. How afraid I was of losing him, how afraid he was of losing the whole world. And
though the tumor was benign, for a long time afterward
I saw an emptiness in his eyes that wasn't filled until after
we sailed here. Something had changed in him, something
I was just beginning to see and understand. A steadier
gaze, a stronger grip, an impatience with unhappiness. It all
deepened when his father died. "There was no warning,"
Paul explained, grieving but also awed and amazed and
grateful. "His expression was peaceful, he'd had no pain."

And for the first time, I saw the violence that struck
me as if I was looking at it through Paul's eyes. A wounded
woman—his wife, his best friend—emptied and terrified.
But alive! Not dead, not dying. She'd survived, she'd out-
witted a killer, she was stronger than she knew and she was
still in his life. The good world and all its foundations had
been shattered, and for so long I saw only ruin. Paul saw
the shards that lay around as materials for rebuilding—
there was still good in them—and the way to discover the

shape of our life was to gather the pieces and try to fit them, one by one.

A flash, stark as a strobe, and I heard the rush of my own blood. Time stopped and I had no words. The afterlife of violence, which would be with me always, had surfaced once again, but before it could pull me under I looked at the glacier: powerful, indifferent, neither malignant nor benign. I looked hard. Its coarse blue-white surface was muddied with rubble and rock. Its face had the appearance of giant crystals standing in formation at the lake's edge. Blue everywhere, and the blue ranged from darkest navy to pale aqua. The glacier had calved recently in crisp, vertical slices, revealing the deep cleft of a brilliant turquoise crevasse.

My back went straight and I stood up, though I didn't know why. The memories and flashbacks and all the reflections that had immobilized me until now were suddenly gone and I was eager to move. I had to.

Zipping up my jacket, I walked toward the visitors center. The tour buses were leaving and I knew the East Loop Trail would be relatively peaceful until the next convoy pulled in. It was quiet. I listened for the complicated whistle of an eagle and heard instead a dull, stuttering creak, like a heavy door swinging on iron hinges.

I looked toward the sound and stopped. A raven stood next to a trashcan, not twenty feet away. The raven's feathers seemed to absorb all the gray midday light, reflecting nothing. It held an apple core in its heavy beak, and against its dull blackness the flesh that clung to the core looked yellow and sweet.

The raven hopped purposefully into the scrub willow at the trailhead and dropped the core. Looking all around, as if to check that no other bird was watching, he picked up a leathery brown leaf—alder, I guessed, decayed from the previous autumn—and with it he covered his treasure. Then he turned my way and cocked his head, inviting me to admire his cleverness, to keep his secret.

EVERYONE AT THE AWARDS POTLUCK looked so clean. Cheeks that had been stubbled were shaved, hair that had been tangled or ignored looked newly cut and styled. There wasn't much anyone could do about the sunburns, though; even the women who wore makeup had bright red noses and ruddy cheeks. I'd tried to tone down the tips of my ears, but they still matched my fuchsia shirt.

As president of the sailing club, Chris hosted the event with his wife at their home in the valley. When I arrived with Tim and Stella, I was a little surprised at the turnout: Skippers and crew brought family, friends, and out-of-town visitors who tripled the crowd we'd been at Warm Springs Bay. The air was a din of voices, a swirl of smiling faces, with Dave—still dressed for the tropics—standing a head taller than the rest. Larry was with his wife Allison, Frank was with Sandy. Mike waved from a group across the deck. Steve was absent, having flown back the day the race ended; "business" was all the explanation he'd offered. I'd barely had time to say goodbye in the shuffle of carrying gear off *Eagle*. I wished I'd had the chance to thank him; he'd taught me a lot about sailing, given me far more than a hat.

"But I sure wouldn't call myself a racer," I said to Allison after confiding in her about feeling seasick during the first leg. "There's so much still to *learn*."

"That's what I liked most about the race," she replied, and smiling back at her I realized that I had too. She seemed as adaptable and good natured as Larry—they were going to be great parents—and soon the three of us were talking about the adoption process they were going through, and then Frank and Sandy joined in, joking about what it was like to come out the other side with their kids grown and mostly gone. And then someone else talked about how everything changes, Juneau wasn't the same with all the cruise ships and tourists, and neither was the weather, come to think of it—unbelievable, almost two weeks in a row of sun. This was the first day the sky promised rain. That was the word everyone used: promised, not threatened.

There was food and more food. Beer and soft drinks in open coolers full of ice, bottles of wine on the tables. We wandered and ate, grazing through the bounty.

At eight sharp, Chris gathered us on the deck for the awards ceremony. Of course *Silver Girl* took the cup. She had finished first in both legs and had corrected out with the shortest elapsed time: forty-two hours, forty-one minutes. How would she have done had her rating been different? No one speculated, not out loud anyway, and the applause was thorough when the trophy was presented.

That over with, spirits warmed up considerably through the rest of the awards. There was good-natured laughter when *Eagle*'s standing was announced: We'd corrected out to sixth place in the second leg. Only two years ago, after all, *Eagle* had won. "How the mighty have fallen!" someone called out. Tim and Frank accepted the ribbing with smiles and shrugs.

Chris waited for us to quiet down before his final announcement. "Yes," Chris said, holding up a shiny red caboose lantern, "this is the award we give last, to the loser. However, this year the loser really isn't!" He was shouting, more from excitement than need; the rest of us were silent. "As you know, *Airloom* came in last on the first leg." We looked at each other and nodded, remembering how she had sailed into Warm Springs Bay over a day behind. "But she continued on to the finish." Chris paused. "And had she started with the rest of us, *Airloom* would have corrected out for the second leg to twenty-one hours!" Whoops and whistles from *Airloom*'s crew. "For that leg, she would have taken first place!"

An explosion of shouting and clapping, of genuine surprise. "Yes!" I yelled with everyone else, made wildly happy by *Airloom*'s success. "Way to go!" The applause couldn't have been longer or louder had she won the entire race. That slow-cruising sailboat had done it. She had tracked, steady as a locomotive, through the rough seas of Chatham Strait. She had defeated *Silver Girl*.

My last memory of that night was the sound of all that cheering, and of *Airloom*'s skipper waving the red lantern high above his head.

THE AIR INSIDE THE PLANE was cool and dry, heavy with the scent of jet fuel. It was a crowded flight

to Seattle; I'd had to search the overhead bins for a space
big enough for my duffle. I plopped into the aisle seat,
clicked on the webbed belt, and closed my eyes.

During the previous night I'd woken at four-thirty,
five-thirty, six-thirty, as if about to go on watch. When I
slept, I dreamed I was moving sail bags into piles, up and
down stairs and ladders. This morning, the bathroom mirror had reflected a face I could only describe as old and
tired: watery, slightly bloodshot eyes set in a mask of dry,
peeling skin. Tiny lines radiated from my weathered lips.

Ten days ago I had flown into Juneau. It felt much longer, as if ten years had been condensed into those days. But
then, time always has taken on a different dimension for me
when I'm on the water. Maybe time *becomes* water, slowed
down, marked by tide and wind, flowing through channels
and back eddies that lead everywhere and nowhere.

So different from the way time passes for me on a commercial airplane. I go up in the air, the earth turns below
me, I come down. I disconnect from one reality, hold myself in a narrow seat for a while, then connect to another.
In between, there is only past time and future time, no *now*.

I listened to the whine of takeoff and felt the moment
of weightlessness as the plane left the ground. The image
in my head wasn't of the stiff fuselage piercing the clouds
but of the wings adjusting like the feathers of an enormous
bird to create a perfect airfoil. I pictured the air flowing
over the curved top, lifting us as invisibly as it lifts a raven
that suddenly opens its wings midtumble in the sky. It is
the curve—of wings and sails—that helps us soar.

Eyes still closed, I thought back on the spectacular

beauty I'd sailed through. *Eagle,* the crew, the teamwork we achieved. I'd liked that: the assigning and perfecting of tasks, the pulling together, the common goal. And—this sounded strange, but I didn't know how else to put it—I'd liked the physical relationship I'd had with those five men. I was there to raise and stow sails, to pull in line, to let it out, to tie it off. At times I was no more than movable ballast to keep *Eagle* level in the water. I was there as a body, as they were, to be trained and directed and ordered about, and I had loved it.

As for my shortcomings—my tendency toward seasickness, my need for more sleep than the others—they were simply there, like my height and weight, which I consider when I raise a sail. Only handicaps if I make them so.

Racing around Admiralty Island reminded me of what I had long known: You use the wind to go forward, even when it's against you. Tack back and forth, resist with the keel, that deep, hidden part of the hull. Pay attention, study the charts and currents, watch the weather. Reduce sail, seek shelter, make repairs—every crew has its limits. But keep going forward.

A FLIGHT ATTENDANT MANEUVERED a metal cart beside me. "Water, please," I said. Nothing else sounded right. I unlocked my tray table and leaned back. Up the aisle, the meal service was beginning.

"Excuse me," said the young woman sitting next to me. "Weren't you at the potluck last night?"

I turned to look at her. When I'd first taken my seat we'd exchanged no more than glances and reflexive smiles.

Our gazes had been fixed inward and back, travelers on a return flight. Now I saw her thick wavy hair, her sun-struck face, her flannel shirt, which was the color of ripe wheat.

"I was. But I'm afraid I can't place you." Of the dozen women I'd met at the layover, I couldn't make a match. The friend of a crew member, I concluded, brought along to the party. "Did you know any of the skippers?"

"John, on *Airloom*," she answered, beaming. "My husband and I were on his crew!"

And I was carried back instantly to that moment when the waving red lantern had filled us all with pride. And back before that, to Chatham Strait, *Eagle* running before the wind; knowing *Airloom* was still in the race had propelled us in a way that competitiveness alone could not.

"That was great last night," I said. The enthusiasm in her face set me sailing; I was moving through water again, my body responding to wind and wave, not to the dull vibration of a commercial jet. "What Chris was saying about the second leg—you must have been flying."

"It was quite a ride, all right. Especially after drifting for three and a half days. But *Airloom* sure is a solid boat, and John really knows how to sail her." She laughed. "He's *still* flying, he feels so good about beating everyone's time, especially that fancy racer."

"*Silver Girl*," I murmured. There couldn't have been two boats more different. Looking back, the mystery wasn't how a heavy-weather boat had outraced the rest of us in heavy weather—all other factors being equal, it was a matter of physics. But all other factors weren't equal.

"What I think is most amazing," I said, "was how you kept going on the first leg." I didn't mention that *Eagle*'s skippers had quit after a day on Frederick Sound; would I have held up myself had I been in charge? *Will* I, for that matter? I pictured myself helping Paul with the house, sanding down the old doors, filling the cracks and holes, repainting—all of it work I'd done before. Nothing new or adventurous. More like standing still. "I mean, there was no wind to speak of. Didn't you wonder if you'd ever get anywhere? Where'd you find the patience?"

"That was the best part!" Her answer wasn't what I'd expected. "I'll never forget those twenty hours we drifted behind Grand Island. John caught a salmon and we had this great barbecue, and then there were whales all around us." Her eyes turned dreamy. "I couldn't have asked for a more romantic honeymoon. I didn't want it to end."

Honeymoon? I watched her twirl the ring on her left hand, listened as she spoke: married two weeks now, her new husband a geologist staying behind to finish a job in Juneau while she flew to her own work in Colorado, where they had met and lived. She talked on about the cabin they were building together, the hiking and kayaking they shared. Speechless, I watched her face as if she were telling me the most wonderful story I had ever heard. It was her story, and *Airloom*'s; Joyce's and Dave's; *Eagle*'s and *Silver Girl*'s. It was everyone's. I was part of a story that no one voice could tell completely, and the knowledge opened me, freed me, woke me to the world.

She didn't even know the gift she was giving me, how the love and hope in her voice made me want to reach for

Paul's hand and squeeze it. What was ahead for us? All
I knew was the bare outline, as unrevealing as the course
description of the Admiralty Island race. I saw *Orca* at the
dock, tugging at the mooring lines, a fair breeze snapping the halyards against mainmast and mizzen. I heard
the rustle of a chart as I spread it open, and the creak of
hinges as Paul opens the hatch, the click of the key and the
engine starting with a rumble.

Paul signals me from the wheel, and I cast off the bow
line. He casts off the stern. Another voyage—it could last
a month or no more than a day. Then another voyage
after that.

The destination is at our feet.

ACKNOWLEDGMENTS

THE STORY OF THE RACE involved more people than I could include in this book. I used the real names of real people in most cases; a few characters are composites. To those who belong here but were not named, I give special thanks, especially to the skippers and first mates of the vessels *Antares, Gipsy, Homespun, Jenn, Jzero, Sea Otter,* and *Shadow.*

I owe much to the Island Institute in Sitka, Alaska. My early drafts first came together during a monthlong fellowship in January of 1997, and their 2001 midsummer symposium propelled me to the finish. Thanks also to the Seattle Public Library Center for the Book, for providing space and solitude for research and writing, and to my colleagues, mentors, and friends at the Dart Center for Journalism and Trauma.

For continuing with me on this long voyage even when the weather turned rough, I thank my agent Elizabeth Wales. Thanks to Dan Weber for his advice at the start, to Christi Killien and Keith Glover for keeping me on the boat, and to Phyllis Hatfield, who never let me quit. Others whose encouragement and honesty kept this book on course were Joanne Mulcahy, Nancy Pearl, Bharti Kirshner, Sheila Bender, Kip Greenthal, Marcia Barthelow, Christine Widman, Cheryl Shaul, Mary Gerstle, Mary Bayley, Claire Meeker, and Marilyn Perry.

Finally, thanks to my companions on *Eagle:* Tim Fullam, Frank Spargo, Larry Tally, Mike Spargo, and Steve Painter.

MIGAEL SCHERER is a Pacific Northwest writer. Her first book, *Still Loved by the Sun: A Rape Survivor's Journal* (Simon & Schuster, 1992), won a PEN/Albrand Citation for distinguished nonfiction and a Pacific Northwest Booksellers Association Award. Since then she has written two more books, *A Cruising Guide to Puget Sound* (International Marine/McGraw-Hill, 1995) and *Sailing to Simplicity* (International Marine/McGraw-Hill, 2000), as well as essays and articles. In addition to her own writing, she is a teacher and consultant for the Dart Center for Journalism and Trauma at the University of Washington in Seattle, and directs the Dart Award for Excellence in Reporting on Victims of Violence.

A Wing in the Door:
Life with a Red-Tailed Hawk
Peri Phillips McQuay

The Barn at the End of the World:
The Apprenticeship of a Quaker,
Buddhist Shepherd
Mary Rose O'Reilley

Ecology of a Cracker Childhood
Janisse Ray

Wild Card Quilt:
Taking a Chance on Home
Janisse Ray

Of Landscape and Longing:
Finding a Home at the Water's Edge
Carolyn Servid

The Book of the Tongass
Edited by Carolyn Servid and
Donald Snow

Homestead
Annick Smith

Testimony:
Writers of the West Speak On Behalf of
Utah Wilderness
Compiled by Stephen Trimble and
Terry Tempest Williams

THE CREDO SERIES

Brown Dog of the Yaak:
Essays on Art and Activism
Rick Bass

Winter Creek:
One Writer's Natural History
John Daniel

Writing the Sacred into the Real
Alison Hawthorne Deming

The Frog Run:
Words and Wildness in the Vermont Woods
John Elder

Taking Care:
Thoughts on Storytelling and Belief
William Kittredge

An American Child Supreme:
The Education of a Liberation Ecologist
John Nichols

Walking the High Ridge:
Life As Field Trip
Robert Michael Pyle

The Dream of the Marsh Wren:
Writing As Reciprocal Creation
Pattiann Rogers

The Country of Language
Scott Russell Sanders

Shaped by Wind and Water:
Reflections of a Naturalist
Ann Haymond Zwinger

THE WORLD AS HOME, the nonfiction publishing program of Milkweed Editions, is dedicated to exploring our relationship to the natural world. Not espousing any particular environmentalist or political agenda, these books are a forum for distinctive literary writing that not only alerts the reader to vital issues but offers personal testimonies to living harmoniously with other species in urban, rural, and wilderness communities.

MILKWEED EDITIONS publishes with the intention of making a humane impact on society, in the belief that literature is a transformative art uniquely able to convey the essential experiences of the human heart and spirit. To that end, Milkweed publishes distinctive voices of literary merit in handsomely designed, visually dynamic books, exploring the ethical, cultural, and esthetic issues that free societies need continually to address. Milkweed Editions is a not-for-profit press.

Join Us

Since its genesis as *Milkweed Chronicle* in 1979, Milkweed has helped hundreds of emerging writers reach their readers. Thanks to the generosity of foundations and of individuals like you, Milkweed Editions is able to continue its nonprofit mission of publishing books chosen on the basis of literary merit—the effect they have on the human heart and spirit—rather than on the basis of how they impact the bottom line. That's a miracle our readers have made possible.

In addition to purchasing Milkweed books, you can join the growing community of Milkweed supporters. Individual contributions of any amount are both meaningful and welcome. Contact us for a Milkweed catalog or log on to www.milkweed.org and click on "About Milkweed," then "Supporting Milkweed," to find out about our donor program, or simply call (800) 520-6455 and ask about becoming one of Milkweed's contributors. As a nonprofit press, Milkweed belongs to you, the community. Milkweed's board, its staff, and especially the authors whose careers you help launch thank you for reading our books and supporting our mission in any way you can.

Interior design by Christian Fünfhausen.
Typeset in 11.5/15 point Requiem
by Stanton Publication Services
on the Pagewing Digital Publishing System.
Printed on acid-free 55# New Leaf EcoBook 100 recycled paper
by Friesen Corporation.